7th e-Learning Excellence Awards 2021

An Anthology of Case Histories

Edited by Dan Remenyi

7th e-Learning Excellence Awards: An Anthology of Case Histories

Copyright © 2021 The authors

First published October 2021

All rights reserved. Except for the quotation of short passages for the purposes of critical review, no part of this publication may be reproduced in any material form (including photocopying or storing in any medium by electronic means and whether or not transiently or incidentally to some other use of this publication) without the written permission of the copyright holder except in accordance with the provisions of the Copyright Designs and Patents Act 1988, or under the terms of a licence issued by the Copyright Licensing Agency Ltd, Saffron House, 6-10 Kirby Street, London EC1N 8TS. Applications for the copyright holder's written permission to reproduce any part of this publication should be addressed to the publishers.

Disclaimer: While every effort has been made by the editor, authors and the publishers to ensure that all the material in this book is accurate and correct at the time of going to press, any error made by readers as a result of any of the material, formulae or other information in this book is the sole responsibility of the reader. Readers should be aware that the URLs quoted in the book may change or be damaged by malware between the time of publishing and accessing by readers.

Note to readers: Some papers have been written by authors who use the American form of spelling and some use the British. These two different approaches have been left unchanged.

978-1-914587-17-7

Published by: Academic Conferences International Limited, Reading, United Kingdom, info@academic-conferences.org

Available from www.academic-bookshop.com

Table of Contents

Acknowledgements ii

Introduction iii

Professional Learning for Online Educators 1
   Orna Farrell, James Brunton, Catriona Ni She and Eamon Costello

Health, Safety and Digital Engagement for Study Abroad 11
   Kate de Blanc, Caroline Kapp, Shannon Krahn and Yeana Lam

Enriching learning whilst reducing staff time through a screencast-based flipped classroom model 29
   Andrew Knight, Jenny L. Mace, Claire O' Brien and Alex Carter

Web-based dementia care partner education using the iGeriCare platform 47
   Anthony J. Levinson, Stephanie Ayers, Lori Mosca, Alexandra Papaioannou, Sharon Marr and Richard Sztramko

OERu: Learning in a Digital Age 61
   Rory McGreal and Wayne Mackintosh

An Online PhD Programme in Computer Science and Information Technology 69
   Izzeldin Mohamed Osmasn

TechTeach in a fully online learning environment 79
   Filipe Portela

Enhancing Student's Practical Skills with Modified Flipped Classroom (MFC) Approach using UFUTURE 101
   Prasanna Ramakrisnan

Coventry University Virtual World Tour 115
   Alex Regan and Albina Szele

Acknowledgements

We would like to thank the judges, who initially read the abstracts of the case histories submitted to the competition and discussed these to select those to be submitted as full case histories. They subsequently performed double-blind evaluations of the entries and made further selections to produce the finalists who are published in this book.

Paula Charbonneau Gowdy is Associate Professor in English as a Foreign Language Teacher Education at the Universidad Andres Bello in Santiago, Chile and formerly Senior Advisor in Learning and Technology to the Government of Canada. Her research interests lie in the sociocultural implications of online learning for teaching, learning and learners.

Reet Cronk is a professor, Associate Dean of Harding Online and Director of Information Systems Graduate Studies. She holds a PhD in Information Systems and a Master of Science in Molecular Genetics. Research interests include the use of technology in education, gamification, e-learning, knowledge management, and the business value of information systems.

Colin Loughlin is the Learning Technology Manager at the University of Surrey (UK) and a PhD candidate with Lund University (Sweden). His research interests are related to large class teaching and the impact of educational theory on classroom practice. Recently published: 'Reclaiming Constructive Alignment' (bit.ly/reclaimingCA)

Susan Crichton is an emeritus professor in Educational Technologies at the University of British Columbia, Canada. She is currently a consultant who has been working to support educators in the K-12 sector, as well as post-secondary trades training and university to respond to the challenges posed by COVID 19.

Introduction

e-Learning and indeed blended learning are now established integral ways in which education and training are managed and delivered across all levels of education and in the workplace. The International e-Learning Excellence Awards provides an opportunity for individuals and groups to consider new and innovative ways of using this method of learning.

The response this year to the seventh international e-Learning Excellence Awards has reflected the continuing innovation being practised in many parts of the world. With 30 initial submissions from 12 countries, 20 competitors were invited to send in a full case history describing their initiative. The range of subjects written about in the case histories has certainly been extensive and the panel of expert judges had their job cut out for them to find the most interesting case histories and short list them to the finalists published in this anthology.

10 authors or groups of authors have been invited to present their work in the final rounds of this competition at the 2021 Virtual European Conference on e-Learning, supported by the University of Applied Sciences HTW Berlin, Germany and as finalists nine initiatives have been published in this book of case histories. The topics to be addressed are listed in the Contents page of this book.

I would like to thank all the contributors to the book for the excellent work which has been done towards developing new and interesting ways of applying e-Learning. And of course, it is also important to thank the individuals who constituted our panel of expert judges.

Dr Dan Remenyi
October 2021

Professional Learning for Online Educators

Orna Farrell[1], James Brunton[1], Catriona Ni She[2] and Eamon Costello[2]

[1]Dublin City University, Ireland
[2]Trinity College Dublin, Ireland

orna.farrell@dcu.ie; james.brunton@dcu.ie; caitriona.nishe@tcd.ie; eamon.costello@tcd.ie

Abstract: This case study describes the experiences of the #Openteach project team in developing a flexible and evidence-based approach to support professional learning for those who teach online. The project targeted online educators in particular. The rationale for this was Continuing Professional Development (CPD) is recognised as crucial to the upskilling of educators to enhance the student learning experience. However, teaching online requires different pedagogical approaches and staff require specific CPD opportunities relating to online learning in order to teach effectively in that context. The #Openteach project sought to address this gap by creating a flexible, online, open access course about teaching online that was grounded in evidence-based practice. The project had a number of phases, which included a needs analysis of online students and educators about effective online teaching, the publication of a literature review entitled Teaching Online is Different, and a pilot evaluation report. The #Openteach open course ran in March 2020 and focused on five key aspects of teaching online: social presence; facilitating discussion; collaboration online; live online teaching; and supporting online students. Following the first run, an evaluation study was conducted to explore and understand participants' learning experiences of the course. Our findings indicate that professional learning about online teaching should be situated online, and the experience of being an online student is invaluable for online educators as it facilitates empathy with students learning in online contexts. Time management and workload are major challenges for educators, therefore professional learning should allow for flexible engagement. Building confidence and reducing the fear of online teaching is an important aspect of professional learning related to online education. Developing understanding and knowledge of online pedagogy is an important element of professional learning about teaching online. Finally, confidence and competence with the tools and technologies for teaching online are important threshold digital competencies for online educators. The #Openteach project has had a significant impact on the professional learning of educators at a number of levels: at a local university level, at a national level; and at an international level.

1. Introduction

This case study details the journey of the #Openteach: professional development for open online educators project, which aimed to develop a flexible and evidence based approach to support professional learning for online educators. The #Openteach: Professional Development for Open Online Educators project, was funded by the National Forum for the Enhancement of Teaching and Learning in Higher Education in Ireland from 2019-2020 and was based in Dublin City University (DCU) in Ireland. The project targeted two groups of educators in particular: part time educators and online educators. The rationale for this was that Continuing Professional Development (CPD) is recognised as crucial to the upskilling of educators to enhance the student learning experience. However, teaching online requires different pedagogical approaches and staff require specific CPD opportunities relating to online learning in order to teach effectively in that context. Additionally part-time educators do not often have access to CPD opportunities. The #Openteach project sought to address these gaps by creating a flexible, online, open access course about teaching online that was grounded in evidence-based practice. See figure 1 below for details of the project communication channels.

Figure 1. #Openteach project channels

2. The infrastructure

The #Openteach project was based in Dublin City University, Ireland. The primary aim of the project was to support the professional development of approximately one hundred online educators working within our fully online DCU Connected programmes. DCU Connected has a thirty-year history of delivering online distance education to mature adult learners. The #Openteach project team was comprised of seven people based in DCU Connected and from a variety of roles and backgrounds: academics, online educators, a learning designer, and an online student.

The #Openteach project targeted DCU Connected online educators, who were both part-time faculty and teaching fully online based in Irish higher education. The cohort of approximately one hundred DCU Connected online educators were geographically dispersed around Ireland and come from diverse backgrounds in academia, industry and teach in a variety of disciplines such as humanities, management, psychology and IT. The cohort had a mix of experienced online educators and novices.

The technical infrastructure adopted in the #Openteach was a wordpress project website, the DCU Moodle site to host the course, H5P and Moodle tools to create content and activities, Videoscribe, Camtasia and Youtube to create and host video content. The Pressbooks platform was used to create the final output, the open book. For research and data analysis purposes, Nvivo, Qualtrics, and Excel were used.

3. Project phases

The #Openteach project had five phases, with each phase producing useful resources (see the figure 2 below)

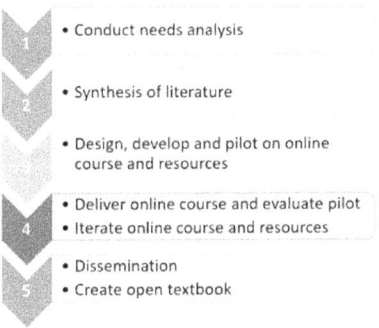

Figure 2. Project phases

groups and several questionnaires. We then produced a report detailing our findings called *An investigation of effective online teaching: a needs analysis of online educators and online students* (Farrell et al, 2019).

Key findings from this report were four key areas that educators identified to enhance through professional development:

1. Technical skills for teaching online
2. Online pedagogy
3. Online facilitation approaches
4. Encouraging online interaction

Then in phase two, we examined the literature around teaching online and conducted a literature synthesis. Following this we published our literature report called *Teaching online is different: critical perspectives from the literature* (Ní Shé et al, 2019). The report examined the literature about online teaching since 2010 and examined the roles and competencies which characterise effective teaching online, as well as approaches to supporting the professional development of online educators.

In phase three, we used the information from the needs analysis report and literature report to begin designing and developing the #Openteach open online course. The course was designed following the ABC Learning design approach, which resulted in a ten hour, fully online professional development course (Ní Shé et al, 2019). You can read more about the design process in our ABC case study. The course focused on five aspects of teaching online: presence, collaboration online, synchronous teaching, asynchronous teaching and supporting online students. The learning outcomes for the course are outlined below in Table 1.

Table 1. #Openteach course learning outcomes

#Openteach course learning outcomes
Demonstrate awareness of teaching and learning pedagogy associated with online education
Facilitate online communication and discussion forums that engage students in learning
Create a supportive community of learners using online teaching pedagogy
Develop and facilitate online collaborative activities that support student learning
Design online teaching activities that encourage student participation and learning and reflect on personal learning from this activity
Use digital tools effectively to support online teaching

The #Openteach course followed a scenario-based approach and participant engagement was largely asynchronous and self-paced as this provided the flexible approach recommended in the literature. The course was designed and delivered on the DCU Moodle site called Loop, and used a variety of tools such as H5P, video, audio, discussion forums, quiz, and workshop in its design (see figure 3 below).

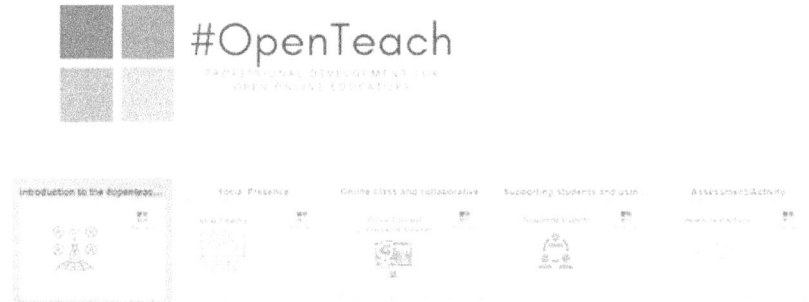

Figure 3. #Openteach Loop course

Phase 4 involved running the course for the first time. The #Openteach online course was free, and participation was open to anyone, from anywhere, with the capability to join an online course. The #Openteach open course ran for the first time in March 2020 with 450 participants and the second time in September 2020 with 557 participants.

In phase five, in order to make the impact of the project sustainable in the long term the project team decided to create a free open access online book using the Pressbooks platform. The book was published in June 2021.

4. Challenges

Over the course of the project, the #Openteach team faced a number of challenges, outlined below.

During the learning design phase, designing credible scenarios that were pitched at the correct level and would stimulate debate and discussion proved challenging. It took several iterations of piloting and testing to develop the optimum scenarios.

When developing the course in Loop (DCU Moodle), we experienced some technical challenges with H5P and achieving a user-friendly course navigation and experience. Further, as we had made the course open to anyone, all those outside of DCU had to manually set up and enrolled in the course, which proved very time consuming. The finishing touches of the course design and development coincided with the Covid-19 pandemic, so the final video assets had to be created at home rather than in a university media studio.

The greatest challenge was that the first run of the #Openteach course coincided with the start of the Covid-19 pandemic in March 2020, which resulted in a much higher number of participants than we had expected, 450. This made facilitating the course much more challenging. We mitigated this by having 5 facilitators and splitting the cohort into smaller groups so as to maintain a high touch facilitation approach. A related challenge was that, again due to the pandemic, a much more diverse cohort joined the course than we had expected. Participants came from higher education, further education, the post-primary sector, and a number of participants came from outside of Ireland.

5. How the initiative was received

Following the first run of the #Openteach course in March 2020, we conducted an evaluation study in order to explore, understand and evaluate its impact on the professional learning experiences of the participants and to inform the iterative design process. The evaluation study adopted a convergent parallel mixed methods design (Creswell, 2014) using qualitative and quantitative methods of inquiry. Data was collected via an online questionnaire (n=101) and via online focus groups (n=10). We then published *The Openteach Pilot Evaluation Report* (Farrell et al, 2020).

In this section, we present a short extract of our findings thematically from the *The Openteach Pilot Evaluation Report* to illustrate how the course was received by participants (Farrell et al, 2020).

When asked if participation in the #Openteach course increased their knowledge of online teaching, 98% of 101 respondents answered Yes, 1% responded no and 1% responded maybe (see Figure 4).

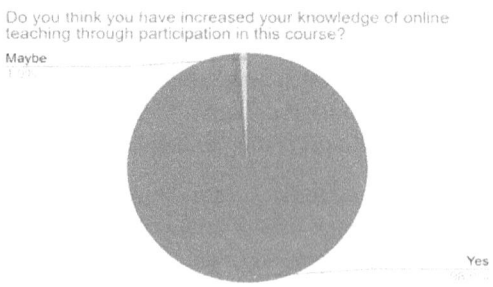

Figure 4. #Openteach impact on knowledge of online teaching

The data indicated that the #Openteach course impacted participants' knowledge and understanding of teaching online in a number of ways:

1. Building confidence about teaching online;

"I had no knowledge of online teaching beforehand and I feel I could teach online with my learners now. I have small groups and individuals so I would be comfortable working online with them now."

2. Developing new knowledge about online teaching including key theories, technology, and strategies for encouraging student interaction;

"I particularly liked the emphasis on pedagogy. The course suited my needs perfectly and allowed me to deepen my knowledge and raise my awareness of the need for carefully designed learning pathways. Online is definitely different to the traditional classroom"

3. Gaining insights into online learning by experiencing it from a student perspective;

"Experiencing a fully online course and seeing the different tips and strategies for engagement in an online environment"

4. Developing ideas and strategies about engaging students in both asynchronous and synchronous environments.

"Suggestions on how to better engage students - specifically some of the suggestions on how to use breakout activities, polls etc. Opportunity to read all the very useful suggestions from others on the course, in the various forums"

5. For those who were teaching online for the first time, the #Openteach course provided them with reassurance, support, and encouragement during a challenging time.

"I am a true beginner so my participation has been limited, but I got a good feel for what is involved in this essential area of teaching"

6. The learning outcomes

The #Openteach project has had a significant impact on the professional learning of educators at a number of levels: at a local university level, at a national level; and at an international level. The project resources and research outputs have been widely disseminated by the project team at national and international conferences. See Table 2 below for details of the project's impact by numbers as of July 2021.

Table 2. #Openteach project impact by numbers

#Openteach Impact by numbers	
Website traffic	33,000 unique visitors, 700,000 hits
Twitter	619 followers, 475 tweets, max impressions 10,779
YouTube	5,300 views
Teaching online is different report	42 citations, 6635 reads
#Openteach open online book	Since published June 21, 956 visitors, 3415 page views
Research publications	5
National conference/workshop	18
International conference/workshop	13
Course participants	1002
Course completers	203

1.1 #Openteach OER

The principle of openness was at the heart of the #Openteach project. All of the resources and intellectual outputs were Creative Commons licensed and openly shared through social media and the project website http://www.openteach.ie throughout the project phases. The #Openteach OER will continue to have impact and support educators long after the life of the project.

7. Plans to further develop the initiative

The project team aims to run the #Openteach course again in 2021 and will further iterate the resources based on feedback from participants and facilitators. Further plans involve the production and dissemination of the research data and lessons learned from the #Openteach project.

8. Conclusion

Over the course of the project, the #Openteach project team learned numerous lessons from the design, development, and delivery of the course and related research. We share these now as our final thoughts. Professional learning about online pedagogy should be situated online, and the experience of being an online student is invaluable for online educators as it facilitates empathy with students learning in online contexts. Participating in and building a learning community contributes positively to the learning experience for educators. Time management and workload are major challenges for educators, therefore professional learning should allow for flexible engagement. Building confidence and reducing the fear of online teaching is an important aspect of professional learning related to online education. In addition, confidence and competence with the tools and technologies for teaching online are important threshold digital competencies for online educators. Finally, higher education institutions need heed the lessons learned from the Covid-19 pandemic, continued investment in online education resources, infrastructure and professional learning is essential to support those teaching online and to prepare for the post-pandemic future which is likely to be far more blended

References

Creswell, J.W. (2014). Research Design: Qualitative, Quantitative and Mixed Methods Approaches. London: Sage.

Farrell, O., Brunton, J., Costello, E., Donlon, E., Trevaskis, S., Eccles, S., Ní Shé, C. (2019). An investigation of effective online teaching: a needs analysis of online educators and online students. Dublin: #Openteach Project.

Farrell, O., Brunton, J., Costello, E., Donlon, E., Trevaskis, S., Eccles, S., Ní Shé, C. (2020). Openteach Pilot Evaluation Report. Dublin: #Openteach Project. (Version 2). Zenodo. http://doi.org/10.5281/zenodo.4599607

Farrell, O., Brunton, J., Costello, Ní Shé, C. (2021) *#Openteach: professional development for open online educators.* Dublin: Pressbooks

Ní Shé, C., Farrell, O., Brunton, J., Costello, E., Donlon, E., Trevaskis, S., Eccles, S. (2019). Teaching online is different: critical perspectives from the literature. Dublin: Dublin City University. Doi: 10.5281/zenodo.3479402

Ní Shé, C., Farrell, O., Brunton, J., Costello, E., Donlon, E., Trevaskis, S., Eccles, S. (2020). DCU Case Study: Using ABC to Design an Online Teaching Course for Open Online Educators. ABC Learning Design Website.

Author's biographies

Dr Orna Farrell is Assistant Professor specialising in online and blended education in Dublin City University (DCU). She holds a PhD in Education from Trinity College Dublin and currently is Head of Open Education, which provides online education to off campus learners.

Dr James Brunton is Assistant Professor and Programme Chair of the DCU Connected Psychology Major programme at Dublin City University, which is an online, open education programme accredited by the Psychological Society of Ireland (PSI). James is a Chartered Psychologist (C. Psychol., Ps.S.I.; C. Work & Org. Psychol. Ps.S.I.; CPsychol BPS) and an EDEN (European Distance Education Network) Fellow.

Dr Caitríona Ní Shé is currently working in Trinity College Dublin as an Academic Developer. Previously she worked on the National Forum's Professional Development of All Those Who Teach priority. Caitríona has worked on several online teaching and technology enhanced learning projects including the #Openteach (online teaching) and the Assessment for Learning (Mathematics resources) projects.

Dr Eamon Costello is an Associate Professor in the Open Education Unit at Dublin City University. Dr Costello holds Doctorate from Trinity College Dublin. Eamon's research interests include Open and Distance Learning, Educational Technology including Virtual and Personal Learning Environments, Computing Education, Open-Source Software in Education and MOOCs.

Health, Safety and Digital Engagement for Study Abroad

The UCEAP Health and Safety Course

Kate de Blanc, Caroline Kapp, Shannon Krahn and Yeana Lam
University of California, CA, USA
ckapp@uceap.universityofcalifornia.edu

Abstract: The University of California Education Abroad Program (UCEAP) annually sends over 5,000 students on international programs. A key component of the predeparture process is preparing students for health and safety, a set of topics that many busy Generation Z students find uninteresting or unrelatable prior to traveling abroad. In September 2019, UCEAP collaborated with dozens of national and international University of California (UC) staff, faculty, students, and program alumni in a multi-phased, highly collaborative workflow to build a new UCEAP Health and Safety eLearning course that would meet the following project goals:

- Empower UCEAP study abroad students to make thoughtful, proactive health and safety decisions before and during travels.

- Clarify roles, responsibilities, and resources that contribute to a healthier and safer study abroad experience.

Infrastructure and technology priorities included designing a secure online experience for students, capturing completion data and feedback, designing with rich visual media and interactivity, and utilizing synchronous-asynchronous collaboration tools with contributors and stakeholder teams. The course launched Fall 2020. Student feedback has been overwhelmingly positive, reporting increased preparedness levels and heightened engagement in course topics such as emotional and mental health, and managing prescriptions and conditions abroad. Evaluation feedback collected through course surveys deployed throughout the student experience indicate initial success in retention of health and safety content, as well as delivery of personally relevant, active learning experiences. Through peer storytelling, health issues are made relatable; through self-paced interactive experiences and realistic scenarios, learners are motivated to analyze, reflect, and choose safe solutions. Gamification through a card game appeals to students' competitive nature and incentivizes student knowledge of common pitfalls. These tactics aid students in retaining and applying key concepts and information once abroad. Further development plans include adding additional features such as student learning journals and decision scenario remediation interactivity; monitoring and updating of accessibility features and health content; and leveraging of existing assets, templates, and instructional strategies for application in staff and faculty trainings internationally.

1. Introduction

The University of California Education Abroad Program (UCEAP) serves all ten campuses in the University of California (UC) system and offers over 150 programs in 40 countries worldwide. Over 5,000 UC students participate n international programs each year through UCEAP while maintaining their status as a UC student and earning UC credit from their coursework. Once a student has been accepted into a program, the UC Systemwide office and campus study abroad offices work to prepare students for their time abroad. One key component of the predeparture process is providing students with health and safety information to help minimize the risk of preventable illness, injuries, theft, or other critical incidents that may disrupt the student study experience.

Despite its importance, health and safety can seem like dull and unrelatable topics to many students as they prepare to study abroad--especially compared to the overall excitement and anticipation of the experience ahead. This lack of interest or relatability can result in students skimming or not reading all the materials provided to them that cover important health and safety information. A further challenge to engagement is that health and safety materials have traditionally been delivered to students in text format, specifically PDF program packets and other text-based online materials that do little to motivate students' interest in learning. A previous version of an online health course was text-heavy and only required for students headed to higher health risk host countries; there was no course specifically designed for all UCEAP students that covered overarching health and safety topics relevant to any program location. These considerations were at the core of UCEAP's motivation to rethink the way these materials are delivered to students, especially considering that lack of knowledge and planning with regards to health and safety can result in severe disruption of the study abroad experience.

To address recurring challenges and increase student engagement in predeparture health and safety topics, UCEAP's Information Technology (IT) team and the International Health, Safety, and Crisis Management (IHSCM) team, along with a robust group of UC system collaborators, embarked on reimagining a new student facing eLearning course, the UCEAP Health and Safety course, in the fall of 2019 that centered on the following project goals:

- Empower UCEAP study abroad students to make thoughtful, proactive health and safety decisions before and during their program.
- Clarify roles, responsibilities, and resources that contribute to a healthy and safe study abroad experience.

- Design the course to stand alone, and work in tandem with other predeparture modules.

Learning objectives presented to students that would meet those goals included the following:

- Create a plan to manage personal health and wellness.
- Apply a framework to research host country laws and norms.
- Determine what actions would support their personal safety.
- Recognize signs of distress and know when to seek help.
- Describe how alcohol and drugs can affect their experience.
- Locate UCEAP resources at home and abroad.

2. The infrastructure

During the data collection and needs assessment phases of course development, UCEAP revisited the internal definition of a student incident: an emergency event that involves one or more UCEAP students, that occurs unexpectedly, and requires an immediate and coordinated response. Documentation of specific recurring incidents that disrupt UCEAP student study abroad experiences (referred to as incident reports) was reviewed to determine stakeholder participation, technology, and pedagogical strategies for delivery. Many seemingly "invisible" factors contribute to disruptions that prevent program participation, interfere with focus on classes, or prevent a sense of student belonging within a program or culture that can quickly escalate into an incident. These factors include emotional and mental wellness, disabilities and impairments, and even a broad understanding of host country cultural norms and laws. Recurring types of incidents identified in UCEAP programs are not unique to UCEAP or the UC system; the FORUM on Education Abroad, a US-based nonprofit that works with government and international partners to maintain Standards of Good Practice in the field of education abroad, produces a yearly 'Report on Critical Incidents' (Forum, 2019) that indicates similar crises and emergencies ranging from illnesses and injuries, theft or crime, behavioral issues, assaults, sexual harassment and violence occur nationally. With the demonstrated need to serve many UCEAP students from multiple UC campuses with high-level health and safety content, plus a requirement from UC Campus Health offices for several additional specific modules for countries that pose higher health risks and vaccination requirements, careful consideration of both the course stakeholder teams and a two-phased agile workflow approach were needed.

The project began with Phase 1 - development of a high-level course for all UCEAP students - which benefited from numerous international collaborators. The stakeholder team for this phase was assembled and launched in September 2019 by the UCEAP International Health, Safety, and Crisis Management (IHSCM) team with input from UCEAP's Instructional Designer. The broad spectrum of stakeholders included UCEAP Directors and study center staff abroad, UC Santa Barbara (UCSB) Student Health staff, and two Campus Administrative Directors from UC Los Angeles (UCLA) and UC Santa Cruz (UCSC). Phase 1 also included ongoing feedback, contributions, and support from staff at multiple UC study abroad offices. Using collected data, agile methodology, and remote collaboration tools, this stakeholder team identified key health and safety topics that would benefit all UCEAP students regardless of their program location. Topics such as mental wellness abroad, managing prescription medications and health conditions overseas, food and water safety, researching a host country's cultural norms, and the relationships between norms and personal safety were some of the topics prioritized by this team. Subject matter experts such as international Faculty Directors and UCEAP alumni were brought in for topical interviews, and staff from the UCSB Resource Center for Diversity, Equity, and Inclusion; the Resource Center for Sexual and Gender Diversity and the UCSB Student Health Drug and Alcohol Program participated in script reviews and feedback exchanges.

Development of Phase 1 continued uninterrupted through the COVID-19 work-from-home mandates, including beta testing with program alumni and nominated students in Summer 2020. The high-level course went live in UCEAP's Learning Management System (LMS) Moodle in October 2020.

Development for Phase 2, which included seventeen country-specific modules for higher health-risk program countries such as Ghana, Costa Rica, and Brazil, launched in September 2020. This stakeholder team consisted of five key members from Phase 1 plus six UC Student Health representatives who contributed medical expertise on health, safety, and vaccination requirements for these modules. The team also contributed to the development of two crucial health-related slides on street food safety and infectious diseases that ended up being transferred to the high-level course to benefit all students in continuously shifting pandemic travel environments.

The complete UCEAP Health and Safety course launched January 2021. In this complete iteration, students complete four modules (high-level) then encounter a map with location pins that enable the students traveling to any of the seventeen higher health risk countries to click their pin and complete the fifth country-specific module. Students are awarded a certificate of completion and answer questions in a brief survey at the end.

The course is a standalone online interactive learning experience authored in Articulate Storyline 360 that speaks a common language, SCORM, with UCEAP's open-source Moodle Learning Management System (LMS). The SCORM format works with the LMS to track interaction, completion, and collect student survey feedback, allowing UCEAP to continuously improve and refine the authored content.

3. The challenges

With existing knowledge of recurring incidents abroad and lack of student engagement with health and safety materials, the stakeholder teams pursued a deeper understanding of the audience that would interact with the content to bridge the existing engagement gaps. Priorities included identifying the audience demographic; determining the range of environments (physical, tech-virtual, cognitive) the audience might be experiencing as they interacted with the content; and examining the knowledge, biases, experiences, or fears the audience might bring to the topics. Learners needed to find relevance in both the material and the delivery and understand the personal benefits of active health and safety decisions over a span of time: from predeparture through the study abroad experience.

Simulated student personas like those used within a User Experience Design workflow were used to examine learner attributes and identify parameters and strategies. The pedagogical design and delivery of content included careful considerations of this demographic:

- UC college students or transfer students, primarily of media-fluent Generation Z.
- May or may not have international travel experience prior to completing the course.
- May be occupied with a full load of classes while applying and while abroad.
- May be extremely busy and distracted, and not eager for more work to do.
- Skills, interests, majors, support systems, physical and mental health conditions, gender identities, ethnicities, sexual orientations, and physical abilities all vary dramatically.

To reach engagement goals most effectively with this target learner demographic, the course design and delivery needed to accomplish the following:

- Establish a welcoming and safe learning environment through visuals, tone, and messaging.
- Acknowledge the range of emotions students might be feeling.
- Present topics through peer-perspective student stories, games, and interactivity.
- Emphasize the personal gain of planning and proactivity.

- Replace text with rich media, infographics, or interactions when possible.
- Implement scenario-based decision assessments that require situational analysis, encourage self-reflection and empathy.
- Prioritize accessible features and inclusive design choices.
- Integrate a printable and downloadable packet of worksheets to represent information in multiple ways and provide a lasting artifact of the most essential course topics.

4. How the initiative was received

Technology, media, and pedagogy work together in the course to help students gain a more comprehensively situated meaning (Gee, 2003), or contextual understanding, of the health and safety content and its personal importance. Opportunity for repetition and practice, immediate instructional feedback, and memorable triggers for self-reflection are implemented through storytelling, interactivity and multimodality, gamification, animation, and decision scenarios. These examples are described below, presented along with student narrative feedback.

Storytelling

Narrated study abroad stories contributed by UCEAP alumni launch essential topics of the course (details are anonymized for privacy). Stories are presented in past tense, through dreamlike video montages and a variety of narrated voices. They are visible, audible, and conceptual hooks to capture attention, also designed as a foundation upon which current students can empathize with a peer experience to transform health or safety information into meaningful, relevant concepts, and action items.

Learning through the perspective of another student makes it more interesting and impactful when going through this course. - Course feedback, UC student, 2021.

I love the stories provided by the students who have studied abroad before. Their experiences are valuable guides. - Course feedback, UC student, 2021.

I liked the stories from past study abroad students. It helped me gain more insight on what could happen while abroad. - Course feedback, UC student, 2021.

Themes and characters in the stories include Ricardo, who reflects on overconfidence and a lack of planning for his food allergy after his bag and medication are stolen in Brazil; Skylar, who, while browsing journals and sketches from studying abroad in Thailand, recalls an unfortunate trip to a Bangkok hospital from eating street food; Lindsay, who reflects on the empathy of a roommate and the benefits of counseling after struggling with mental and emotional wellness adapting to Sweden's cold and dark winter; and Alix, who reflects on researching cultural norms and making personal safety decisions from the perspective of a queer student studying in Morocco. In the case of Alix, their story draws a connection between two seemingly unrelated data sets (Collins, 2016): one consisting of data about host country cultural norms (to be researched by the student), and the other pertaining to knowledge about personal safety. This connection between safety and cultural norms has proven to be a recurring challenge for many UCEAP students studying abroad. The peer perspectives provide an authentic entry point for new or discordant concepts to be situated into broader situations and contexts, creating triggers that are easier to recall and act on.

Interactivity and Multimodality

Students are constantly surrounded by devices and platforms that offer short, varied activities and natural-feeling interactions. These interactions combine text, imagery, and streaming rich media within unified visual packages. The UCEAP Health and Safety course considers learners' experiences with this variety, unity, and pace through the breadth of instructional activities curated slide to slide. The customized interactions are presented through clean branded layouts, encouraging the learner to manipulate content through buttons and sliders and reflect on revealed images, text, choices, and feedback. The interactions build on and support other narrated, textual, and visual learning content, while requiring attentiveness and action to progress from one activity to another. Students report that interactivity and variety help maintain engagement and prevent tune-out or multi-tasking.

I liked how interactive it was; the slider, cards, pie chart, and short quizzes. It made me pay a lot more attention to this course. - Course feedback, UC student, 2021

I liked that it was interactive, so it forced me to pay attention. - Course feedback, UC student, 2021

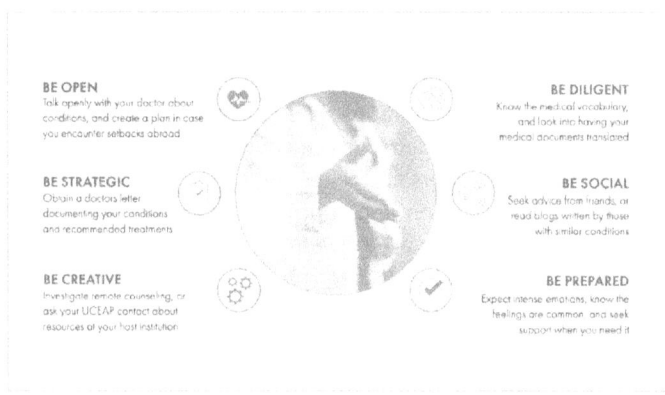

Figure 1. Animated instructional content, peer storytelling, and click-and-reveal interactions.

Printable PDF course worksheets provide another dimension of multimodal interaction to the online course. The worksheets are designed with branded icons from the course, combined with minimal text and ample white space, to encourage learners to add their own content. During the course orientation video, learners are audibly and visibly prompted to engage with the worksheets: to print the PDF and make lists, take notes, or doodle during the online course; or alternately, since the PDF exists initially in the digital space, bookmark or save the worksheets in a folder for later. Both choices result in an artifact summarizing the important content discussed in the course that can act as a memory trigger or a reference tool.

I liked the pdf that we could use to take notes and follow along because otherwise, I would forget the information. - Course feedback, UC student, 2021.

I enjoyed the worksheets and printable documents which I can refer back to. - Course feedback, UC student, 2021.

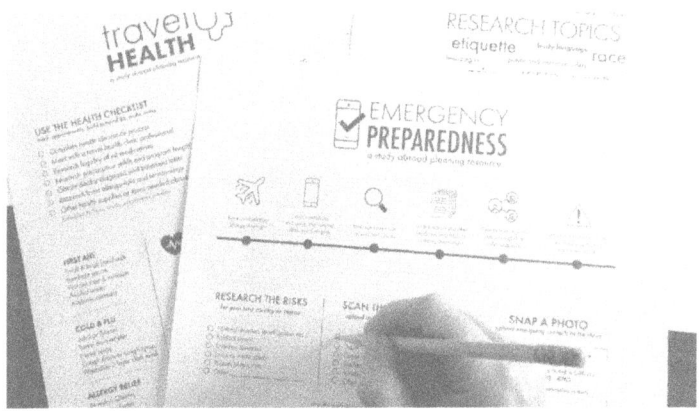

Figure 2. Printable course worksheets for multimodal engagement.

Gamification

A skeptical learner persona prompted the development of a gamified pre-assessment. This skeptical persona has prior travel international experience, or assumes they already know study abroad health and safety; they may carry a bias that an online health and safety course will be a waste of time. The stakeholder team examined ways to acknowledge this persona's prior experience as well as strategies to tap into any biases about the course and shift them towards relevance and personal gain.

A card game greets students in the course orientation. The activity, which is built with animated effects, audio, and click-and-reveal functionality, playfully challenges a learner to correctly answer a series of Fact or Fiction statements related to health, safety, and studying abroad. Six different cards present different statements (one on each card), and the learner makes a choice for each card based on their current knowledge. Through this activity, the learner is provided an opportunity to reflect about how much they already know, or think they know, about health, safety, and studying abroad prior to engaging in any course topics.

Fact or Fiction statements include commonly misunderstood topics of studying abroad, contributed by the Phase 1 stakeholder team. Examples:

"Campus-based disability accommodations will automatically transfer to your host institution abroad." Fact or Fiction?

"If you break a local law in your host country, the US Embassy can get you out of jail." Fact or Fiction?

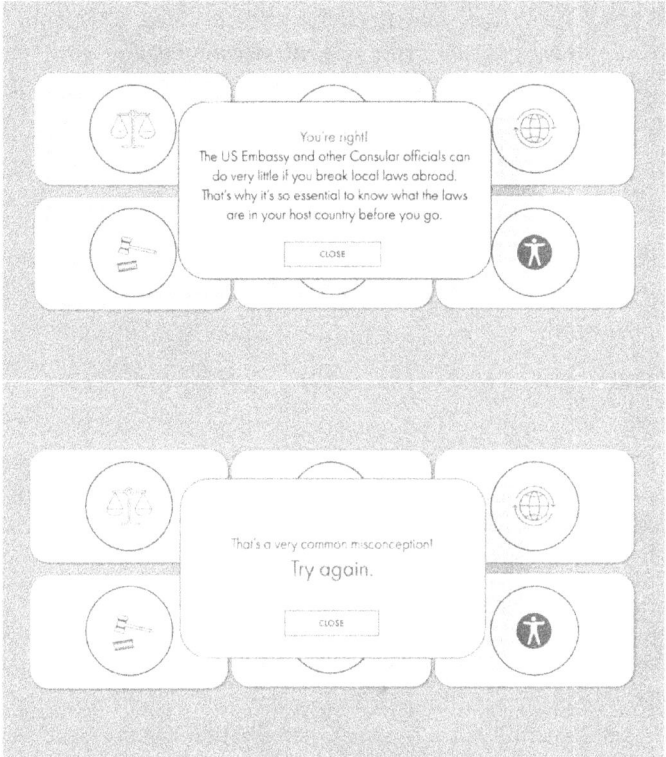

Figure 3. Example card game and feedback in course orientation.

If a learner gets the answer right, the card flips around to display positive feedback such as *Nice job!* along with a descriptive summary of why the topic is important to consider. The feedback also confirms they will gain even more expertise by continuing. The reward of getting an answer correct can boost confidence levels, providing incentive to continue, overcome more challenges, and master more details.

Those who choose incorrectly are encouraged to *Try again*, triggering feedback such as *That's a very common assumption!* The process of choosing fact or fiction and receiving this feedback promotes learner reflection not only about what they thought they knew, but also the validity of course topics reframed as learning targets (Guskey & McTighe, 2016) that can help learners avoid similar misconceptions and overcome obstacles in their upcoming experience. Through this gamified interaction, a skeptical student or seasoned traveler who might have assumed they knew everything they needed to know can receive lighthearted, clear signals about what they are about to learn; signals that also clarify the personal gain involved. This understanding of personal gain can boost both curiosity and intrinsic motivation in the concepts and information the course discusses.

> *I liked the fact or fiction game and its user interface. It provided short and concise answers to important topics to be covered.* -UCEAP alumni, 2020.

> *Gamifying an experience and acknowledging that I might have previous knowledge is a good move.* - UCEAP alumni, 2020.

> *I'm kind of competitive, so I was very determined to get it right.* - UCEAP alumni, 2021.

Decision scenarios

Students engage with four decision scenarios throughout the course. Scenarios are designed to encourage intermittent recall, reflection, and analysis of the health and safety topics within realistic study abroad contexts. In these activities, the learner makes decisions based on the presented contexts, and receives immediate explanatory feedback about those decisions.

In one scenario, the learner receives a voicemail message from a friend, Jiwon, who is asking for advice about how to plan for disability accommodations and prescriptions during predeparture. To provide this advice, one must reflect on health processes, timelines, and medical action items from previous slides, encouraging more active organization and integration of the new information (Moreno & Mayer, 2007). Another scenario begins with a realistic situation of a group going out to a local club in Madrid. In this scenario, the learner analyzes which decisions made throughout the evening were the safest, such as staying with a larger group, or ensuring they left the dorm with a fully charged phone. Best practices in emergency preparedness and signs of mental or emotional distress are also recalled and reinforced in decision activities.

Like the gamified card game, those who select wrong answers in these scenarios are provided encouraging feedback and context in preparation for another try; the scenarios embody an approach that mistakes can provide useful learning experiences when paired with immediate feedback (Clark & Mayer, 2012). These interactions allow unlimited tries with guiding feedback about their choices until the healthiest or safest option is selected.

> *The small checks for understanding at the end of each section were very helpful for me.* - Course feedback, UC student, 2021.

I liked the interactive-ness of the course; the ability to interact with the scenarios that play out during events that may suddenly occur. - Course feedback, UC student, 2021.

The scenarios were realistic and helpful to put myself in certain situations. - Course feedback, UC student, 2021.

5. The learning outcomes

Well over 800 UCEAP participants are abroad or will soon be abroad this Fall. Learning outcomes are being measured and evaluated through the following overarching strategies:

- Interviews with UCEAP program alumni beta testers
- Post-course survey feedback from students, prior to studying abroad
- Mid-term survey feedback from students currently abroad (Fall 2021 cohort)
- Post-program survey feedback from student returnees (Fall 2021 cohort)
- Incident report data comparisons dating back to 2016-17 academic year

Interviews were conducted with recent program alumni who beta tested the course. Alumni were asked to recall their state of mind and perceptions of health and safety during predeparture; to reflect on the challenges or surprises they experienced abroad; and to provide feedback about course design, activities, and engagement levels. In these interviews, alumni:

- Recalled feeling a lack of motivation to read health and safety materials during predeparture
- Described the gamification, stories, and course interactivity as extremely engaging
- Identified cultural norms, mental and emotional wellness, and travel insurance as specific topics most likely to benefit future students

Post-course survey feedback from students has been overwhelmingly positive. This qualitative feedback, collected through a four-question built-in course survey, indicates that the UCEAP Health and Safety course is delivering personally relevant, engaging learning experiences. After completing the course:

- 91% of students reported increased confidence in making health and safety decisions for themselves after completing the course
- 91% of students reported increased knowledge on how to access UCEAP health and safety materials at home and abroad after completing the course

Student narrative feedback articulated heightened engagement in course topics such as emotional and mental wellness, travel insurance, and cultural norms. Storytelling is mentioned frequently as a course activity that makes the health and safety topics relatable, and the decision scenarios are described as realistic activities that are helpful in encouraging self-reflection.

Mid-term survey data is being actively collected from the first cohort of students studying abroad after the pandemic travel restrictions. Thus far, 35 students have responded to the brief survey on their perceptions of knowing and applying course knowledge, as well as their perceptions on preparedness. Nearly two-thirds (63%) of these mid-term survey respondents reported they have made informed personal safety decisions that benefited them and have located relevant program documents and policies in the UCEAP portal. Early data from this cohort also indicated that a majority of students expressed confidence across the personal and health wellness topics covered in the course, including managing one's mental health, knowing emergency protocols, and knowing the cultural norms of one's host country. Students were most confident in applying knowledge in food and beverage safety and avoiding infectious diseases. Variations in ratings, for example, between infectious diseases and cultural norms (see Figure 4) could point to adjustments and emotions that students commonly experience mid-program as well as suggest a potential area for further assessment and attention.

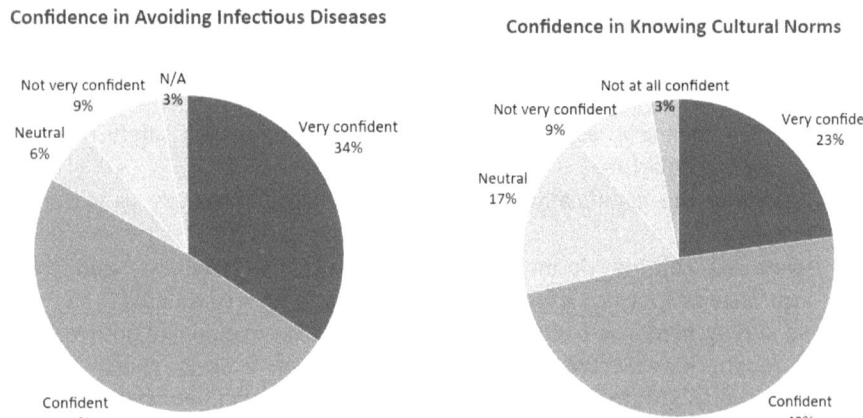

Figure 4. Ratings of student confidence in example personal health and wellness topics.

Some preliminary comparisons were made on the perceived level of preparedness between the mid-term respondents who took the course and previous Fall cohorts at the end of their program who did not take the online course. These results showed somewhat similar ratings in cultural adaptation (77% prepared or very prepared for mid-term vs. 79% for previous Fall cohorts) but higher ratings of perceived health and safety preparation for the mid-term respondents who took the online course (86% vs. 74% for previous Fall cohorts). Caution must be exercised in drawing conclusions from these preliminary comparisons since the surveys were administered at different points of the student life cycle. The complete midterm dataset will be run against the upcoming post-program survey feedback when these same students return home from their experiences. Their post-program survey feedback could also then be compared with feedback from previous cohorts.

Finally, data on incident reports function as a metric for measuring change in student behavior over time. Although not all critical incidents can be averted, one of the project goals is to promote thoughtful student decision-making, which may have the effect of reducing avoidable reported critical incidents. Comparisons of incident report data prior to and after the launch of the course could provide some evidence for course effectiveness.

As the first cohort of UCEAP participants abroad signals that more UC students will be participating in study abroad programs, the importance of better preparing UCEAP program participants for health and safety is evident. UCEAP continues to evaluate feedback from student surveys, from UC Health Staff, and from International Health, Safety and Crisis Management incident reports to measure and evaluate effectiveness of this course over time.

6. Plans to further develop the initiative

All UCEAP students now benefit from a comprehensive online health and safety course, not just students headed to higher health risk host countries, and the benefits are already apparent from the learner feedback. Plans for course improvements include:

- Create a remediation option in all decision scenarios to prevent multi-attempt burnout
- Design course topic improvements as indicated by patterns of student survey feedback
- Add learning journals that allow students to type printable notes after completing modules
- Improve ease of keyboard navigation and screen reader functionality in specific interactions
- Deploy health edits and additions per UC Student Health and the UCEAP IHSCM team
- Leverage successful templates and instructional strategies in new UCEAP course designs

Other notable developments emerging from the initial successes of the UCEAP Health and Safety course include formation of a new student-focused learning outcomes committee that ties directly into UCEAP's strategic goals, mission, and vision. The committee is integrating learning outcomes initiatives into the study abroad cycle: not only predeparture preparedness but also aspects that can enhance in-country learning and achievement such as goal setting and mile posting, frameworks for increasing intercultural communication skills, and building professional development and career guidance opportunities upon return. These topics have emerged as increasingly prevalent in student and alumni feedback during course development. Future initiatives will continue to facilitate a more positive and thorough student study abroad experience--all building on known learning and engagement formats, strategies, and successes of the UCEAP Health and Safety course.

References

Clark, R. C., & Mayer, R. E. (2012). Scenario-based e-learning: Evidence-based guidelines for online workforce learning (1st ed.). Pfeiffer.

Collins, S. (2016). Neuroscience for learning and development : How to apply neuroscience and psychology for improved learning and training. Kogan Page.

Gee, J. P. (2014). What video games have to teach us about learning and literacy (2nd ed.). Macmillan.

Guskey, T. R., & McTighe, J. (2016). Pre-assessment: promises and cautions. Educational, School, and Counseling Psychology Faculty Publications, 17. https://uknowledge.uky.edu/edp_facpub/17

Moreno, R., & Mayer, R. (2007). Interactive multimodal learning environments. Educational Psychology Review, 19 (3), 309–326.

The Forum on Education Abroad. (2020). Report on Education Abroad Critical Incidents (No. 2019). https://forumea.org/wp-content/uploads/2021/04/2019-CID-Report.pdf

Author Biographies

Kate de Blanc works as an analyst on the International Health, Safety, and Crisis Management team for University of California Education Abroad Program (UCEAP). Prior to working for UCEAP, she worked for the National Park Service and the Monterey Bay Aquarium in educational capacities.

Caroline Kapp is an instructional and visual designer whose extensive background of creative media design and higher education teaching yield a learner-centered approach to designing eLearning solutions for the University of California Education Abroad Program (UCEAP).

Kate de Blanc, Caroline Kapp, Shannon Krahn and Yeana Lam

Shannon Krahn is an Institutional Research Analyst and the Grants Coordinator with the University of California Education Abroad Program (UCEAP). Shannon manages grants and awards projects and their workgroups, applying institutional research, policy analysis, and building customized data tools to support UCEAP, academic departments and the entire UC system.

Yeana Lam is a research analyst at the University of California Education Abroad Program (UCEAP). Her current research focus is on the academic integration of study abroad and the assessment of intercultural learning, cognitive skills, psychosocial skills, and other learning outcomes in education abroad activities

Enriching learning whilst reducing staff time through a screencast-based flipped classroom model

Andrew Knight[1,2], Jenny L. Mace[1], Claire O' Brien[3] and Alex Carter[4]

[1]Centre for Animal Welfare, University of Winchester, Winchester, UK
[2]Department of Academic Quality and Development, University of Winchester,
WinchesterUK, Nathan Campus, Griffith University, Nathan, Queensland, Australia
[4]Lexica Films, Eastleigh, UK
Andrew.Knight@winchester.ac.uk
Jenny.Mace@winchester.ac.uk
Claire.OBrien@winchester.ac.uk
lexicafilms@gmail.com

1. Novel solutions to potentially overwhelming challenges

In 2016 one of us (AK) was asked to establish a new MSc in Animal Welfare Science, Ethics and Law at the University of Winchester, UK. This is a rapidly-developing discipline, with many higher educational programmes now established within the UK and abroad. Unlike all competitor institutions offering similar programmes, however, we lacked an on campus animal collection, such as a zoological collection, farm or laboratory animal vivarium. We were provided with only one other faculty member along with AK, to establish two degrees (this MSc, and a related undergraduate degree). Neither had previously established new higher educational programmes, and these two faculty members lacked an established reputation in the animal welfare field. Jointly, this comprised a set of potentially overwhelming challenges.

A conventional approach would likely have resulted in predictable outcomes – we would have struggled to successfully draw students from more established and better-resourced competitor institutions, and our new programmes would have struggled to survive. Such circumstances warrant unconventional, innovative approaches. This case study describes the use of multiple approaches that have been unconventional and innovative at our University, and within our academic discipline.

To overcome the challenges created by lack of a live on campus animal collection, AK decided to create an entirely distance learning (DL) MSc programme, in which guided readings within our virtual learning environments (VLE) would be completed by textual summaries, embedded images and videos, weekly webinars in all modules, and online discussion fora. Students would participate in or submit a considerable variety of assignments, through our VLE or the wider internet, including submission of academic posters, and remote presentations recorded as movies and uploaded to YouTube.

Such an entirely DL programme provides exciting opportunities to educate students around the world. However, it is challenged by communication barriers including those associated with VLEs, internet connectivity and asynchronous time zones. To fully realise the potential of DL, we must design platforms, content and educational activities to maximise student engagement and accessibility (Bayram, 2013). Masters level students are often busy, professional people. Maximising their satisfaction also requires resources that are quick and easy to use.

Our programme was innovative both within our field, and at our University. It proved very attractive, recruiting students worldwide, and rapidly developed a strong reputation in our field. Student satisfaction and performance was good. In the three years from 16/17, headcounts rose by 41% annually. During recruitment for the 20/21 academic year, enrolment projections spiked, one point reaching 246% of the previous year's level. Much as we like to think this was due to the success of our programme, we acknowledge the major role likely played by significantly increased interest in DL programmes, in a pandemic-focused world.

Despite its success, our programme was not without flaws, of course. Ever since our 2016 inception, we had delivered largely the same one-hour webinars annually in all modules, based around unenriched PowerPoints. Students in webinars have been reluctant to engage, and there is little time in any case, after delivery of didactic teaching content. Variable internet connectivity meant that webinars were mostly audio only, which was more reliable. In the 2018 programme evaluation survey a student commented that they: "… would like to actually see the lecturers rather than just listen to them. … a short video within a lecture would be good."

Additionally, dramatic rises in student numbers to very high levels, with no increase in staffing (due to University financial constraints), meant that by academic year 19/20, marking workload was barely tenable. Staff engagement on weekly discussion fora had dropped to zero, despite the significant importance of discussion fora within DL programmes. Our dissertation supervision had become less than optimal. We had become victims of our own success. With sharply rising student numbers, and continued denial of additional staffing requests, significant change had become necessary to ensure academic workloads remained viable, and to prevent further deterioration of the student experience.

Flipped classroom model

After consultation with students and his Programme Team, AK decided to transition our MSc toward a flipped classroom model, piloting this in a single animal welfare module. He had experience with the flipped classroom approach at his previous University.

In the flipped classroom model, didactic teaching content is provided prior to timetabled lecture sessions, via modalities such as pre-recorded PowerPoint presentation videos (screencasts), notes and readings. Pre-recorded videos tend to be more stable than live webinar video. Prior provision of didactic teaching content frees up timetabled sessions for more interactive 'live' learning activities, in which the learning focus shifts from understanding and remembering information, to application, analysis and evaluation (Figure. 1). This can enhance critical thinking and higher level problem solving skills (Francl 2014). These are particularly important within our discipline of animal welfare, which includes numerous controversial social issues, which require the application of knowledge, analysis and critical reasoning.

Evidence indicates such more interactive learning exercises can increase student engagement and attendance, knowledge comprehension and retention, and student satisfaction (Deslauriers et al. 2011, Charles et al. 2012, Francl 2014, Hwang et al. 2015).

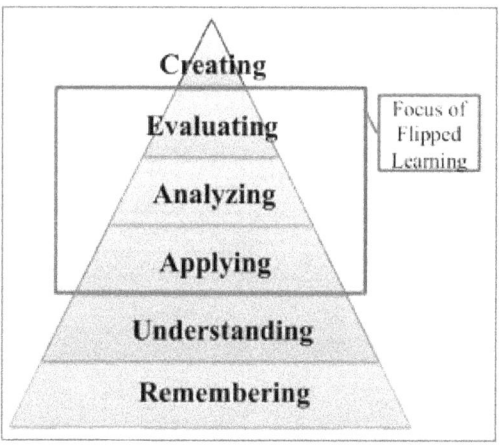

Figure. 1. Educational objectives of in-class activities for flipped learning (Hwang et al. 2015).

Prior to timetabled 'live' learning activities, optimal provision of didactive teaching content requires online learning environments that are interactive and personalized. This enables self-paced knowledge acquisition, at times and locations convenient to the user (Zhang et al. 2006).

We provide readings, textual summaries, still images and links to external videos, but our enriched screencast videos comprise the heart of our didactic information provision. Screencast videos provide a powerful and expressive way to capture and present information (Hampapur and Jain 1998). Video provides a multi-sensory learning experience that improves information retention (Syed 2001), and is especially helpful for visual learners (Bargeron et al. 2001) (Figure. 2).

Figure 2. Video provides a multi-sensory learning experience that improves information retention. Adapted by Yousef *et al.* (2014) from Dale (1969).

Several studies have indicated that learning outcomes of e-learning with instructional videos can equal or improve upon those achieved by traditional classroom learning (e.g., Bento 2000, Hiltz and Turoff 2002). Hence, as Charles et al (2012) ask, "in an era with a perfect video-delivery platform ... why would anyone waste precious class time on a lecture?"

Learning is optimised when tools offer interactivity and flexibility to meet learner needs. The 'cognitive learning model' notes that a learner's attention is limited and therefore selective: "If learners can determine what to construct or create, they are more likely to engage in learning (Shang et al. 2001)."

Through this model, our objectives were to provide a more enriched, engaging and effective student learning experience, and to increase student satisfaction, whilst concurrently saving staff time.

2. Development and implementation

We discussed our planned approach at staff-student meetings, and piloted it from the start of 2021, over one semester. We aimed to provide enriched screencast videos of short (~ 20 minute) durations, with contents clearly signposted. This would allow easy topic selection, allowing the user to determine what to study, at times and locations convenient to them. This should optimise student satisfaction (Khalifa et al. 2002).

Creation of enriched screencast videos was not an area in which we had prior experience and required us to overcome several challenges. First, we were challenged by lack of any existing university software well suited to screencasting, and by our lack of knowledge of software options. However, one of us (AC) was engaged as a videography consultant, to survey and assess the range of software options. The most suitable and affordable were Screencast-O-Matic (USD 48/yr) and Doodly (USD 67/yr) (Figures. 3 - 4).

Figure. 3. 'Screencast-O-Matic' comes with a stock video library.

7th International e-Learning Excellence Awards

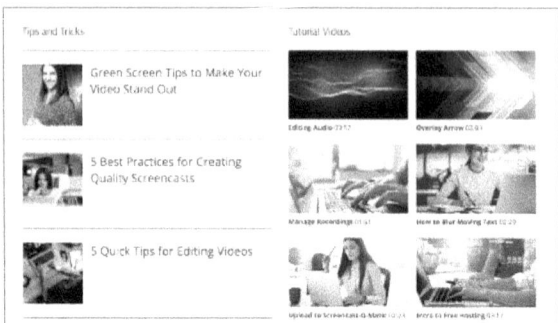

Figure. 4. 'Screencast-O-Matic' provides numerous tutorials to help users quickly create engaging, professional videos.

AC produced a report (Fig. 5) assessing the strengths and weaknesses of each, with costings information, for both personal and university-wide licences.

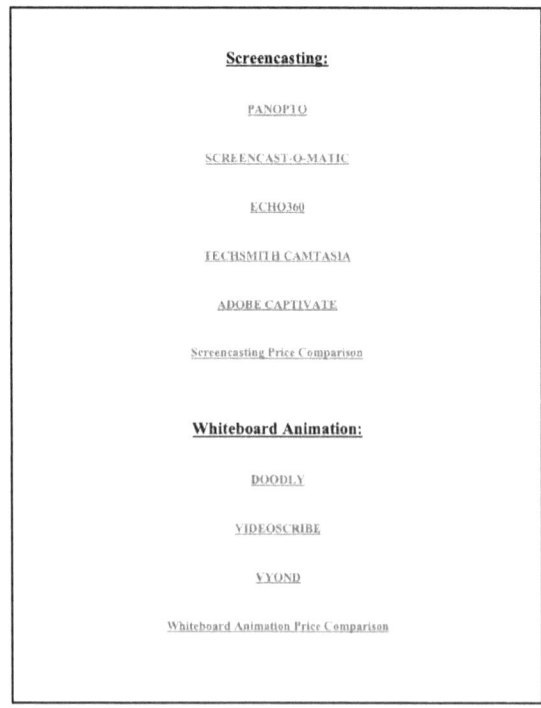

Figure 5. We prepared a detailed report on screencasting and animation software options.

We were also challenged by our personal inexperience utilising the software. We anticipated this would also be a challenge for most academics who might wish to follow in our footsteps. Accordingly, AC also prepared a simple, user-friendly guide to screencasting using the chosen software.

To implement our plans, one of us (JM - Module Leader) would implement the flipped classroom model with guidance from AK and AC. During the 2021 spring semester JM used and refined the user guide, to create enriched screencasts within an animal welfare module. These comprised PowerPoint presentation videos (screencasts) of around 20 mins, enriched with embedded webcam video of the lecturer, other illustrative videos, animations, and interactive polls and quizzes (Figure 6). These screencasts were interspersed with readings, and with quizzes to test knowledge acquisition, highlight problem areas, and increase engagement. An important question included at the end of every week, was 'Do you have any questions relating to this week's material?'

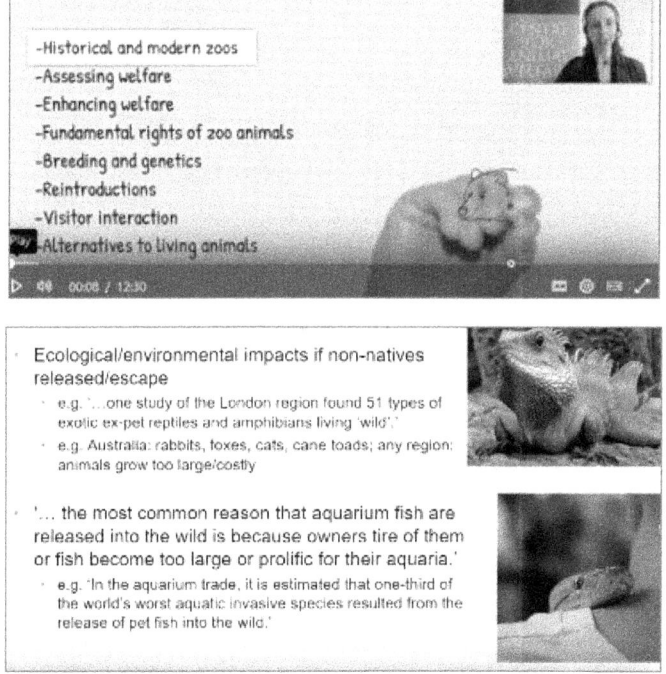

7th International e-Learning Excellence Awards

Figure 6. Webcast slides with embedded animations, images, videos and polls/quizzes.

Each week, Lecturer JM reviewed results from embedded polls and quizzes (Figure 7) and reviewed the most common questions raised by student relating to that week's taught material. These were then addressed during follow-up live sessions, held every two to three weeks during semester.

3. Resultant student experience

Annual surveys of student experiences were conducted within all modules, and for our MSc overall. This year, some extra questions were added, asking about experiences with our new screencast-based flipped classroom model. Our survey response rate for this module was 37% (13/35), which was broadly consistent with response rates in all other MSc modules this year (27% - 40%). Our overall programme survey response rate of 26% (9/35) compared with a range of 38% - 46% in the previous three years.

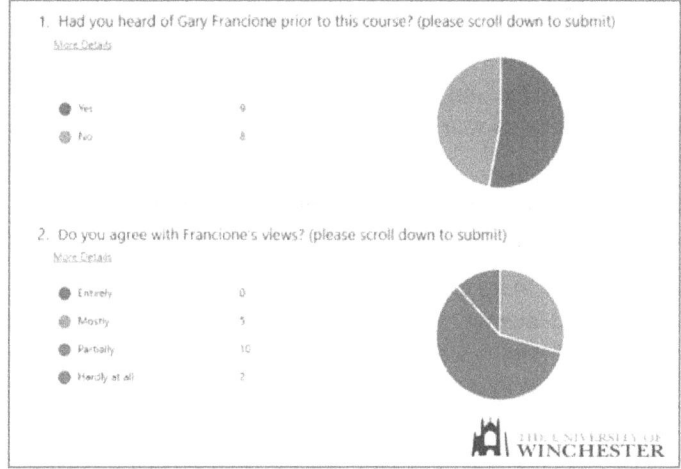

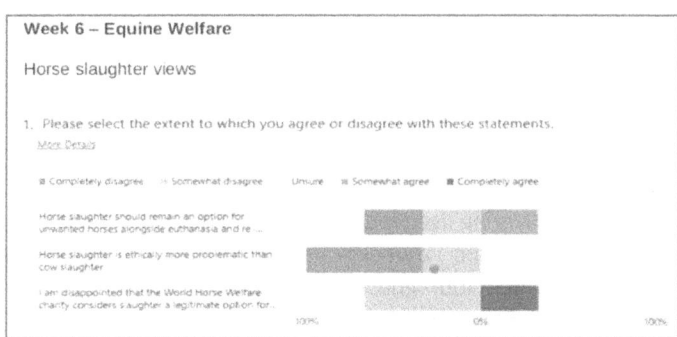

Figure 7. Results from polls and quizzes embedded in videos.

Overall, the new teaching model was very well received. Combined student feedback from our programme and module surveys indicated common themes (Table 1).

Table 1. Common themes identified among programme and module survey respondents, concerning our new flipped classroom teaching model.

Some preferred live sessions, but more preferred the new model
Most felt the new model did not hinder learning or impact assignment performance
Flexibility of the new model was popular, and decreased pressure
Some felt learning to be 'more immersive and engaging than the previous term and enables more opportunities for discussion/interaction with staff and other students'
Questions embedded within pre-recorded screencasts were appreciated

Some students were more able to manage their workloads, because these were more flexible, enabling self-paced study:

> "Having pre-recorded lectures available allows flexible learning where required or a concentrated session so it provides choice" (Garratt 2021, pers. comm.).

> "I like that you can pause or rewind to go over again", and "I prefer this way of doing things, it gives me time to think. [Previous one hour] lectures can be quite full on" (module evaluation feedback).

> "I just wanted to say that I am really enjoying the new style of lectures. Makes me feel a little less overwhelmed and more interactive! The splitting of the lesson into three 20-minute videos has not only held my attention for longer but allows me to digest the information better. ... due to constant distractions in my household I would usually end up breaking concentration and forgetting a lot of information from the beginning of lectures. It was also quite daunting when it came to revising for exams to do the 1-hour lessons in one go plus the reading. Overall, the shorter videos with the commenting and the little bits of reading in between the videos have helped me feel less overwhelmed, and I really appreciate that. When Andrew first sent the message out that lecture styles were changing, I was sceptical, but the small difference to learning style has made quite a big impact!" (Barnes 2021, pers. comm.).

Time previously used delivering live webinars was re-purposed to substantially enrich the student experience over the 12 weeks of semester. Building on pre-existing guest speaker plans, we provided four guest speakers, three Q&A sessions focused in questions arising following each week's screencast videos, one topical discussion/debate using breakout rooms, and one focused on assignments. Most proved popular, especially the topical discussion/debate, with multiple requests for more (Table 2).

Table 2. Student feedback following a topical discussion/debate using breakout rooms.

'Thanks Jenny, this was really great!'
'Was a good session! Really enjoyed listening to everyone!'
'I really enjoyed this tonight!'
'Thanks everyone for this brilliant session!'
'The topical discussion was enjoyable and a great idea - it makes you think in a different way when you have to work in a team, discuss live and feedback views - very interactive and good life skills to practice.'

4. Student learning outcomes

Formal student surveys were twice conducted late in semester. Responses to the module evaluation survey were encouraging (Table 3).

Table 3. Percentage of respondents who definitely or mostly agreed with Module survey statements.

92	Content is intellectually stimulating
100	Learning and teaching approaches are interesting and engaging
100	Module has provided opportunities to explore ideas or concepts in depth
77	Module has provided opportunities to apply what I have learnt
77	I have had opportunities to ask questions about, and discuss, my work
92	Resources for this module support my learning effectively
100	The information I need is available to me on this module

Assessment outcomes were also positive and have increased slightly compared to the previous three years (Table 4), although it must be noted that there was also an assignment change in 2021 which may also have affected these results.

Table 4. Average module grades from 2018 - 2021.

2021	69
2020	60
2019	65
2018	60

One indicator of student engagement is page views within the VLE. These were broadly similar to those of the previous years (Figure 8).

Figure 8. Average Virtual Learning Environment page views over the semester from 2021 (top) to 2018 (bottom).

We also sought informal feedback throughout the semester. Some students felt enabled to participate more: "I must say the recoded [webinars] are very good and I especially like that they are interactive, asking about our opinions etc. I am mostly quiet during the webinars (cannot really explain why 😊) but this new type of webinar actually motivates me to participate which is very nice!" (Vasileva 2021, pers. comm.).

Interaction similarly increased in discussion fora: "… the discussion forum was much more fun this semester. Knowing that what we write will actually be read and commented by others … was a real incentive to participate! I think, this module was actually the nicest of the whole course for me! Very demanding but in a good way." (Module evaluation feedback). Another commented, "… more opportunity for student interaction. This really makes us feel part of the course and this semester is wonderful because there is so much opportunity provided to interact with peers!"

One student did report missing the social 'chat' during live webinars. We supported student organisers to establish regular 'virtual coffee breaks' using our VLE, advertising these to all students. These proceeded fortnightly and helped to overcome some of the isolation experienced by our DL students. After an initial 'faculty free' period of 45 minutes, faculty are routinely invited to attend. We do so on an ad hoc basis. Conversation often turns to teaching and assignments. These sessions have proven their worth, helping build links between students and faculty as collaborative partners in the learning process, and providing an important additional communications channel in which we often discuss problems students may be having, answer questions, and provide important advice about forthcoming assignments.

Finally, we also assessed our new teaching model against University of Winchester teaching 2020 objectives and strategic priorities. The University 'Approach to blended learning' has asserted the importance of varied teaching activities, manageable workloads, flexible, self-paced study, and interactive opportunities. Our screencast-based flipped classroom model achieved all of these objectives. It allowed greater diversity of live teaching activities. Students were more able to manage their workloads, which became more flexible, enabling self-paced study. These appear to have optimised student learning and enhanced student satisfaction.

5. Recommendations

Similar to many institutes, ours is a relatively small, teaching intensive university, that currently receives minimal external funding. Accordingly, faculty are commonly heavily loaded with teaching duties. These preclude innovation and creativity, and the development of novel teaching innovations and solutions to problems. Despite best efforts, this inevitably impacts student experience and performance. Heavy teaching workloads also severely curtail faculty efforts to develop their research and knowledge exchange portfolios.

Programme rollout and delivery

These challenges are not limited to universities like ours and will be well understood by most experienced higher education faculty. However, the screencast-based flipped classroom teaching model we developed offers major potential to free up faculty time normally spent annually preparing for and delivering live webinars or lectures. Time demands are largely limited to preparation of the initial screencast set, in the first year, and to updates. In the first year, some additional time must be invested, as enriching screencasts with embedded videos, images, animations, polls and quizzes, does take additional time. However, the process becomes smoother with experience. To limit the impacts of additional time requirements in the first year, and to mitigate the potential for student opposition to more wholesale changes, a limited, manageable proportion of courses should be changed to the screencast-based flipped classroom teaching model, every semester. After this is done, faculty time requirements are primarily limited to updating teaching content, and to organising optional, extra teaching sessions. With respect to the former, the use of shorter 20-minute videos, rather than entire lectures, facilitates quicker, easier editing, or if necessary, re-recording. Flexibility of future screencast usage can be maximised by avoiding mention of specific dates or specific content ordering (e.g., '... in week 2'), in favour of more generic terms (e.g., 'as discussed in the week focused on X').

Some students are understandably concerned about potential impacts on their learning and experience, of loss of live interaction in webinars. This should be managed in several ways. First, the previous learning experience should be enriched, through the provision of extra live sessions. Numerous options are available. In our case we offered guest speakers, class discussion/debate of controversial topics, assignment preparation sessions, and Q&A sessions focused on questions most commonly raised or otherwise important, harvested from quizzes at the end of weekly screencasts. We also put extra time into engaging with students in discussion fora, providing a richer experience in this domain. Online discussion fora, e.g., focused on weekly teaching content, are particularly important for increasing engagement, and identifying and addressing comprehension problems, in distance learning programmes.

It is important to allocate sufficient time to clearly describe and explain the extra sessions and discussion fora engagement that may be offered, and then to deliver consistently on these. We found that Initial scepticism of some students reversed, when they experienced the increased flexibility offered by the pre-recorded screencasts, and once they had the chance to participate in the extra learning and engagement opportunities.

Students offered a range of additional, enriched, learning experiences, still have to cover all of the original learning content. Accordingly, to prevent student overload–another potential sources of student dissatisfaction–we recommend limiting the number and time required by extra sessions, and also keeping them optional, as we did.

Technical considerations

Many academics will not have experience preparing enriched, pre-recorded screencasts; nor will be particularly IT-savvy. Hence any software chosen for this purpose for use by academics at large, should be as user-friendly and reliable as possible. It should also allow basic video editing. As mentioned, we chose to use Screencast-O-Matic, partly because it also includes a stock video library. The latter can be helpful, although videos in the public domain may also be used, with acknowledgement of the source.

Also important, are setting up a good recording environment. These include using a good quality webcam (at least 720p HD quality), an uncluttered background, good lighting on your face and avoidance of shadow, a good quality external microphone that plugs into the recording computer, and a quiet room. Finally, some practice is obligatory, prior to commencement of screencast recording.

6. Future plans

Our screencast-based flipped has been a major programme enhancement for our 100% DL MSc. We have substantially enriched learning, optimised engagement and satisfaction, and preserved or enhanced learning outcomes, without any additional staffing. This approach has been innovative at our university, and within our field.

Within our 2021 programme survey, 100% of question respondents expressed a wish to see our screencast-based flipped classroom approach continued, and 71-86% would like it implemented in various additional modules. We plan to steadily implement this within additional MSc modules. However, the initial time investment is considerable; hence this will occur at a manageable rate, over years, refining the process as we go.

We are keen to encourage and support colleagues within and outwith the University, interested in creating their own customised versions of our approach. Our software review and screencasting software guidance booklet (Fig. 16) are available from the authors. It has been designed, with stepwise screenshots, to be as clear and simple as possible, for academics unfamiliar with screencasting. Other, free options, such as Open Broadcaster Software, also exist, and will continue to emerge. To encourage and guide colleagues, we've provided presentations summarising our screen-based flipped classroom teaching model, on several occasions at our own University, and others, and are seeking opportunities to present it more widely, facilitated, of course, by remote presentation technology. We also plan to publish our model and recommendations within appropriate journals.

Figure 9. Our user guide to creating enriched, pre-recorded videos, using our recommended software.

Acknowledgement
The development of this educational innovation was supported by a University of Winchester Learning and Teaching Innovation Fund grant.

References
Bargeron, D., Gupta, A., Grudin, J., Sanocki, E. and Li F. (2001). Asynchronous collaboration around multimedia and its application to on-demand training. In *Proceedings of the 34th Annual Hawaii International Conference on System Sciences, Hawaii, USA*. NY: IEEE.

Bayram, L. (2013). Enhancing an online distance education course with video. *Procedia-Social and Behavioral Sciences*, 83, 463-467.

Bento A. (2000). Developing a class session using audio and video streaming. In M. Khosrowpour (Ed.), *Web-based Learning and Teaching Technologies: Opportunities and Challenges*, Hershey, PA: IGI Global. 103–116.

Prober, C. G., and Heath, C. (2012). Lecture halls without lectures—a proposal for medical education. *N Engl J Med*, 366(18), 1657-1659.

Dale E. (1969). *Audiovisual Methods in Teaching*. NY: Dryden Press.

Deslauriers, L., Schelew, E., and Wieman, C. (2011). Improved learning in a large-enrollment physics class. *science*, 332(6031), 862-864.

Francl, T. J. (2014). Is flipped learning appropriate? *Journal of Research in Innovative Teaching*, 7(1).

Hampapur, A., and Jain, R. (1998). Video data management systems: metadata and architecture. In W. Klas and A. Sheth (Eds.), *Multi-media Data Management*. New York: McGraw-Hill.

Hiltz, S.R. and Turoff M. (2002). What makes learning networks effective? *Communications of the ACM* 45(4), 56–59.

Hwang, G. J., Lai, C. L., and Wang, S. Y. (2015). Seamless flipped learning: a mobile technology-enhanced flipped classroom with effective learning strategies. *Journal of Computers in Education*, 2(4), 449-473.

Shang, Y., Shi, H. and Chen S.-S. (2001). An intelligent distributed environment for active learning, *ACM Journal of Educational Resources in Computing*, 1(2es), 4.

Syed, M.R. (2001). Diminishing the distance in distance education. *IEEE Multimedia* 8(3), 18–21.

Yousef, A. M. F., Chatti, M. A. and Schroeder, U. (2014). The state of video-based learning: A review and future perspectives. *Int. J. Adv. Life Sci*, 6(3-4), 122-135.

Zhang, D., Zhou, L., Briggs, R. O., and Nunamaker Jr, J. F. (2006). Instructional video in e-learning: Assessing the impact of interactive video on learning effectiveness. *Information and Management*, 43(1), 15-27.

Author biographies

Andrew Knight is Professor of Animal Welfare and Ethics, and Founding Director of the Centre for Animal Welfare, at the University of Winchester; a European, UK, American and New Zealand Veterinary Specialist in Animal Welfare; and Principal Fellow of Advance HE. He established a 100% distance learning MSc in 2016.

Jenny Mace is an Associate Lecturer within the University of Winchester's Centre for Animal Welfare. She is a Fellow of Advance HE. Her co-authored paper on an animal welfare topic, is published in the journal *Animals*. She is currently focusing on much-needed research into backyard chicken rescue/care.

Claire O' Brien is a TEL Developer & Trainer at the University of Winchester since 2019 after lecturing for four years. She specialises in how the growing use of technology in higher education affects pedagogical practices and the use of digital technologies in supporting learning, teaching, and assessment.

Alex Carter is a filmmaker and writer from Southampton, with degrees in Film Production and Creative Writing from University of Winchester. Alex has produced over 40 educational videos for the University's Centre for Animal Welfare, working under the name Lexica Films, and is co-founder of disability access organisation Autek CIC.

Web-based dementia care partner education using the iGeriCare platform

Anthony J. Levinson, Stephanie Ayers, Lori Mosca, Alexandra Papaioannou, Sharon Marr and Richard Sztramko
McMaster University, Canada
levinsa@mcmaster.ca; stephanie.ayers@machealth.ca; lori@machealth.ca; papaioannou@hhsc.ca; marrs@mcmaster.ca; sztramko@hhsc.ca

Abstract: Most people living with dementia rely heavily on informal family care partners to provide support. Many national and global recommendations highlight the importance of education that helps care partners develop knowledge and education to support themselves and a person with dementia in living well. While web-based interventions have been shown to be effective, few high-quality web-based care partner dementia education programs are freely available in both English and French. We designed and built the iGeriCare.ca web-based dementia education program. The free, open-access program was co-developed by experts in dementia care and e-learning at McMaster University, with extensive input from care partners. It was developed using best practices in evidence-based instructional design for multimedia learning and funded through peer-reviewed grants. It consists of 12 multimedia lessons, as well as email-based subscription learning and over 25 monthly live-streamed Q&A events with subject matter experts. The goal of iGeriCare is to improve care partner knowledge and self-efficacy; as well as to raise awareness of strategies and services to improve their quality of life. Since launching in July of 2018, there have been over 157,400 unique visitors to the site, with extensive use of the lessons and videos of the live events. A multimodal approach to evaluation has used a variety of surveys as well as key informant interviews. Feedback has been consistently positive for all components, with visitors identifying various ways that the education is having a helpful impact. A qualitative study with key informants suggested the development of an educational prescription app and other strategies to incorporate the resource into clinical workflows. The Canadian Institutes of Health Research (CIHR) funded the French translation, which was launched in June 2021. Further dissemination and study of iGeriCare is planned as well as research on care partner impact; as well as adapting it for health care worker training.

1. Introduction

The prevalence of dementia is increasing, and more family/friend care partners will be involved in caring for people living with dementia. Despite their key role, many care partners may have little knowledge of the disorder, community resources, or the caregiving role. Numerous quality standards all highlight the importance of education that helps care partners develop knowledge to support themselves and a person with dementia in living well.(Ontario Ministry of Health and Long Term Care, 2016; Health Quality Ontario, 2018; Canadian Academy of Health Sciences, 2019; Public Health Agency of Canada, 2019) Providing evidence-based education to help care partners better understand dementia, its progression, treatment options, and available supports can be challenging to do in the clinical setting; time and resource constraints can impede a health care provider's ability to participate in education. Although several education programs currently exist, they vary in availability and often lack flexibility to accommodate the realities of caregiving; additionally, care partners in rural communities may have little to know no access to dementia specialists and therefore limited opportunities for face-to-face education.

Internet-based care partner interventions have emerged as a potential solution to address some of these challenges. A recent needs assessment outlined that care partners were actively seeking trustworthy sources of information about dementia on the internet.(Ringer *et al.*, 2020) Various systematic reviews suggest that web-based interventions may result in a range of improved health outcomes for care partners, including reductions in depression, stress, distress and anxiety.(Ploeg *et al.*, 2018; Sherifali *et al.*, 2018; Deeken *et al.*, 2019; Zhao *et al.*, 2019) Other studies have identified that greater public education is needed for care partners, and improved mechanisms are needed for busy clinicians to provide care partner education.(Peterson *et al.*, 2016)

We developed iGeriCare (igericare.ca), a multimodal e-learning intervention to help educate family care partners of people with dementia.

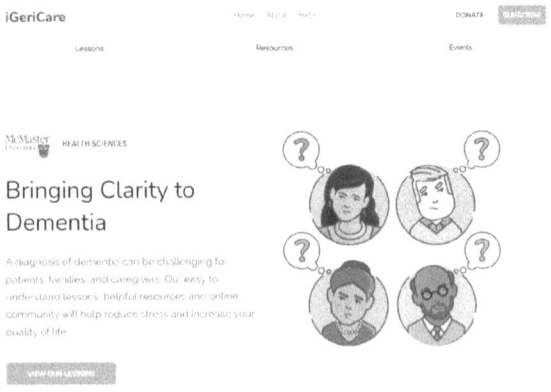

Screenshot from the iGeriCare home page.

Anthony J. Levinson, Stephanie Ayers, Lori Mosca, Alexandra Papaioannou, Sharon Marr and Richard Sztramko

It was developed by experts in dementia and online learning, as well as family care partners, to help meet the needs of care partners by improving their knowledge and self-efficacy, as well as raising awareness of strategies and services to improve their quality of life and that of the person with dementia. The core content consists of 12 asynchronous, multimedia lessons on a variety of topics such as 'What is Dementia?', 'The Stages of Dementia', 'Caregiver Wellness', and lessons related to treatments, psychiatric syndromes, responsive behaviours, and safety in the home.

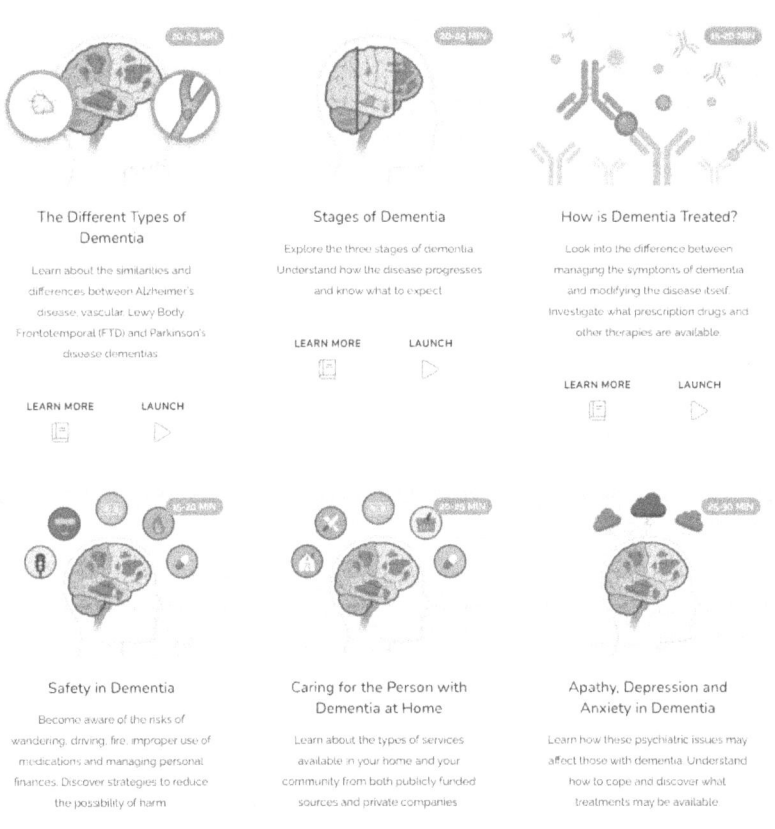

Screenshot from the iGeriCare lesson aggregator page.

iGeriCare also provides an array of curated resources, a series of weekly 'micro-learning' emails with small segments of content to reinforce material from the lessons (subscription learning), and monthly web-streamed live online events that allow participants to post questions to subject matter experts. These events are recorded, and the videos made available on the site. The asynchronous and fully online elements of iGeriCare have proven even more valuable during the pandemic, when face-to-face approaches have been unavailable. Directing patients and care partners to the site is easy to implement for clinicians and is an efficient and cost-effective way to address dementia care quality standards.

2. The infrastructure

Drs. Anthony J. Levinson and Richard Sztramko are the co-creators of iGeriCare. Dr. Levinson is an Associate Professor in the Department of Psychiatry at McMaster University (Hamilton, Ontario, Canada), John R. Evans Chair in Health Sciences Educational Research, and Director of the Division of e-Learning Innovation. He is an expert in neuropsychiatry, dementia education, online learning, and technology-enhanced knowledge translation. Dr. Levinson has extensive experience with the design, development, implementation, dissemination and evaluation of consumer health education resources and e-learning. Dr. Sztramko practices both Geriatrics and General Internal Medicine at St. Peter's, Hamilton General, and Juravinski Hospitals in Hamilton, Ontario, Canada. He is an Assistant Professor at McMaster University, and focuses on eHealth interventions related to patient education, physician and healthcare provider communication, and home health monitoring. He is passionate about leveraging technology to create value for patients, care partners, and healthcare workers. Additional members of the multidisciplinary product development team also include a project manager, programmers, designers, a marketing specialist, a research coordinator, and other subject matter experts. The team included lived-experience care partners, as well as nurses, case managers, and additional geriatricians with expertise in dementia.

Our program is unique when compared to other care partner educational resources because it is one of the few web-based dementia care partner interventions to incorporate best practices in multimedia e-learning instructional design, it is free/open-access, and includes asynchronous lessons and email-based microlearning. To our knowledge, it is also the only asynchronous multimedia e-learning dementia education program that has a French translation available. Key components of the instructional design include: use of the principles of multimedia learning and audio narration; personalization, including the use of a virtual 'coach'/embodied instructional agent; segmenting the content into manageable topics to reduce cognitive load; authentic scenarios and worked examples; interactive review questions; and learner control over navigation.(Clark and Mayer, 2016)

Anthony J. Levinson, Stephanie Ayers, Lori Mosca, Alexandra Papaioannou, Sharon Marr and Richard Sztramko

Each lesson in the intervention follows a similar structure - lessons begin and end with a vignette and conclude with multiple choice or true/false questions to reinforce learner knowledge. Learners can complete lessons in any order; however, lessons are designed to build upon each other. iGeriCare follows many Clark and Mayer multimedia principles and best practices for e-learning. The Multimedia Principle recognizes that people learn more deeply from words and relevant graphics than from words alone; iGeriCare lessons use both relevant graphics and audio narration to communicate content.(Clark and Mayer, 2016)

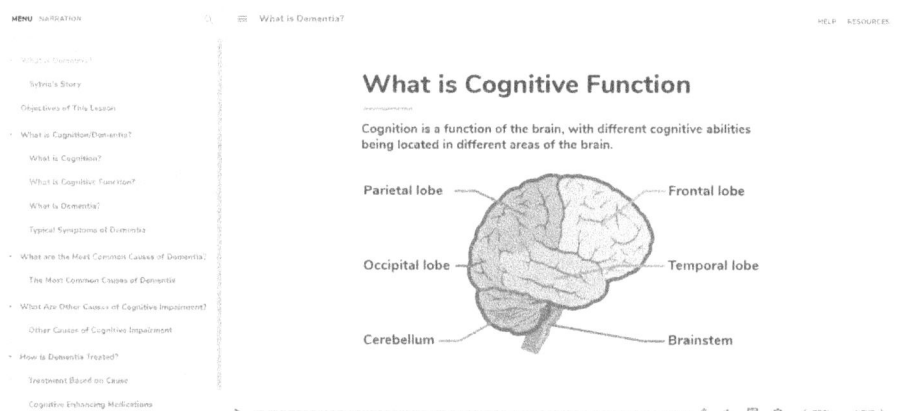

Screenshot of iGeriCare lesson demonstrating Multimedia and Contiguity Principles.

iGeriCare lessons are designed so that spoken words and graphics are used to best advantage, which aligns with the Multimedia Principle. Consistent with the Modality Principle, audio narration is used throughout, with decreased on-screen text to reduce redundancy and cognitive load. Instructional graphics are designed to align with the Contiguity Principle; labels on illustrations are kept next to the structure they are labelling.(Clark and Mayer, 2016)

The Coherence Principle encourages the minimization of irrelevant cognitive load imposed on memory during learning.(Clark and Mayer, 2016) To adhere to this principle, the iGeriCare lessons ensure that there is no extraneous audio or graphics, and that narration per slide is generally less than 2 minutes (without any distracting background music, for example).

Clark and Mayer identified that people learn more deeply from multimedia lessons when learners experience heightened social presence; they refer to this as the Personalization Principle.(Clark and Mayer, 2016) The iGeriCare lessons use audio narration in a conversational style with a virtual coach or avatar to help meet this recommendation.

The Segmentation Principle states that people learn more deeply when content is broken down into small chunks, and learners can control the rate at which they access the chunks.(Clark and Mayer, 2016) iGeriCare content is divided across multiple lessons, and within each lesson is a table of contents that learners can use to continue or replay sections.

Additionally, during the design and development of the lessons and website, an iterative, participatory instructional design and development methodology - the Successive Approximation Method - was used, with extensive involvement and review from a range of experts in dementia care, including care partners.(Allen and Sites, 2012) There were several phases to the development and evaluation:

1. Extensive expert review of each lesson by three geriatricians and two case managers, and review by two family care partners of people living with dementia, with iterative updates. Prototype lessons that were closely approximated to the final user experience were evaluated using the Quality in Use Integrated Measurement (QUIM). (Seffah et al., 2006) The QUIM consists of 10 factors and subsequent overlapping criteria. It was chosen because it encompasses a comprehensive list of usability components and factors; it also allows for qualitative feedback and enables a fluid and natural interview script (Seffah et al., 2006). During this phase, expert and care partner review found that the information was highly relevant/helpful and was segmented into manageable amounts of learning. They also valued the colour and design of the e-learning screens, the meaningful use of images, and the clarity of the terminology.
2. In-person usability testing of the iGeriCare website by three family care partners of people living with dementia. Usability testing was informed by Krug's best practices for pragmatic user testing (Krug, 2014). A think-aloud approach was used to gauge user experience and usability. Participants emphasized the importance of 'trusting and knowing' the source of the information (i.e., trusting of McMaster University and dementia subject matter experts/physicians). Participants also enjoyed the look and navigation

of the site, specifically commenting on ease of task completion. No major usability issues were identified during this phase of testing.
3. Evaluation of the iGeriCare website and e-learning lessons by 5 family care partner participants. The final phase to the development and evaluation included measuring the initial feasibility and effectiveness of iGeriCare. Additional outcomes of interest included quality of life and burden. (Ware and Sherbourne, 1992; Zarit et al., 1980) Overall, iGeriCare was perceived positively with the participants reporting that the website and lessons were easy to navigate and follow. Despite the small sample size, a statistically significant improvement was found in two of the quality-of-life survey sub-domains: social functioning (SF-36; $p=0.03$) and general health (SF-36; $p=0.02$). Although not a statistically significant improvement, a trend in improvement in burden was seen post intervention (ZBI; $p=0.09$).

In terms of the technologies employed, the iGeriCare website is built using the Laravel 8.0 framework, hosted on cloud servers running PHP 7.4. The French translation was incorporated using the Laravel-Translatable package by Astrotomic. Google analytics is used for web analytics. Multimedia lessons were built using Articulate Storyline 360 and hosted on Amazon's Web Services (AWS) platform. Initial iterative reviews and feedback of the lessons used the Articulate 360 Review platform. A custom wrapper written in javascript collects user data for slide views, lesson completions and ratings and sends these events through an API to be stored in a MySQL database. An administrative dashboard for viewing the data and reports was built using Laravel Nova. Live online events were initially recorded in a studio using the Mevo camera and live streamed through Facebook, with the recordings hosted on Vimeo. During the pandemic, events switched to the Zoom web conferencing platform, but with the same approach for streaming and hosting recordings. Subscription learning via email was deployed using the Mailchimp marketing platform for automated email campaigns. Feedback surveys for various components of the project use the SurveyMonkey platform.

3. The challenges

Several challenges were encountered during the project, with a variety of approaches to address them. At a high level, the key challenges that led to the project itself relate to the challenges for busy clinicians to be able to provide patient and family care partner education efficiently and effectively within the time constraints of the clinical encounter. The second high-level challenge related to the lack of freely available, bilingual, high-quality, multimedia e-learning about dementia for care partners. While many web-based initiatives have been developed for research studies, few of these resources are freely available for use by clinicians and care partners.

In terms of more specific e-learning challenges, because many of the target audience of care partners are older adults, we wanted to employ design principles that were very user-friendly, particularly for older adults. Specific design decisions were made during development to reduce user burden and challenges. Account creation, log-in, and password requirements were removed to allow for ease of access. The website interface was designed to maintain simplicity for the user experience. While lessons employ multimedia and interactivity, we deliberately tried not to have too much interactivity within the lessons that might add more complexity to the user interface and experience. Email-based subscription learning was also added, as email is a technology that many older adults are familiar with. The live events are streamed as videos to reduce the burden on users having to learn how to use a separate web conferencing platform. Viewers can participate in live events via the iGeriCare website or Facebook and have multiple methods through which they can submit questions or comments to participate.

The convenience of removing account creation and login/authentication also presented us with a challenge with respect to more detailed analytics related to lesson metrics. This was overcome through the use of a custom tracking solution using JavaScript on the slides with lesson-related metrics (slide views, time on slide, lesson completion, lesson ratings).

Live events were initially broadcast and recorded in person, which became impossible during the pandemic. This challenge was overcome by switching to Zoom for the events.

Promotion and dissemination remain a challenge, but we have used a variety of methods to raise awareness including digital media marketing techniques, organic promotion, stakeholder engagement with key dementia care experts and organizations (so-called 'intervention agents'), media appearances, and word-of-mouth.

While web-based education may be an effective intervention, little is known about how best to implement it in various family care partner education settings. To better understand implementation in various settings, we conducted semi-structured interviews with a number of key stakeholders. Using transcripts of these interviews, we performed a qualitative examination to identify recurrent themes, including facilitators and barriers, that might inform organizations' planning and implementation efforts with respect to web-based dementia care partner education.(Levinson, Ayers, *et al.*, 2020) We found that opinion leaders in dementia care were generally enthusiastic about implementing high-quality web-based dementia care partner education. As a result, we have increased the dissemination of collateral promotional materials, continued engagement with various champions and intervention agents (such as physicians, Alzheimer Societies, long-term care homes, and others), and continued ongoing multimodal strategies for implementation. We also developed somewhat innovative collateral marketing materials such as educational prescription pads that clinicians could use to 'prescribe' particular lessons for patients or care partners, as well as pilot testing an educational prescription web-based app.(Levinson, Bousfield, et al., 2020)

Funding also remains a challenge, and we continue to pursue research grant opportunities as well as donations. The lead co-creators continue to volunteer their time for the initiative. Opportunities to generate revenue from related products (e.g., paid courses for health care workers) are in development.

Making available a French version of the program was addressed through grant funding, strategic partnerships with collaborating francophone organizations, and supplemental technical solutions within the Laravel framework.

4. How the initiative was received

Launched in July 2018, to date there have been over 222,500 user sessions, with over 157,400 unique visitors; the iGeriCare lessons have had over 37,100 views. iGeriCare was promoted using digital marketing with paid ad campaigns for both the public and healthcare professionals. The campaigns were evaluated using cost per click data and event tracking data from Google Analytics, allowing us to assess the conversion rate (i.e., the number of lessons started) by acquisition source. Website usage data from Google Analytics was analyzed and reported monthly to evaluate website usage, visitor behaviour, engagement, and acquisition channels.

User satisfaction with the website, lessons, and live events are assessed using customized online surveys on the SurveyMonkey platform to gather qualitative and quantitative data, including Net Promoter Scores (NPS). The NPS is a management tool that can be used to gauge customer satisfaction; it asks respondents their 'likelihood to recommend' a product or service based on their experience on a scale from 0-10.(NICE Satmetrix, no date; Graham et al., 2012) The NPS is calculated by classifying respondents into the following categories: 'detractors' (rated 0-6), 'passives' (rated 7-8), and 'promoters' (rated 9-10) and calculating the percentage in each group. The percentage of detractors is then subtracted from the percentage of total promoters to give the final NPS score which can range from -100 to +100. The overall Net Promoter Score for iGeriCare lessons is 65. iGeriCare's NPS scores would be classified as 'great' and demonstrate high rates of satisfaction. It greatly exceeds the industry averages, and strongly suggests that many users will be repeat visitors and enthusiastically recommend iGeriCare to others. Feedback from the live events indicates that users value the information provided and the opportunity to ask experts questions. The NPS for iGeriCare's live events is 70; which would be classified as 'excellent.' The archived videos have been watched over 3,100 times by 1,120 unique viewers since the live events launched. To date, there have been 2,478 subscribers to our email list, and 1,481 subscribers to the micro-learning email program. Emails have a 51.1% open rate and a 9.0% click-through rate, which far exceeds industry standards. The micro-learning email program has a NPS of 50, which is classified as 'great.'

Some samples of free text comments about the lessons include:

> "Thank you sincerely for the excellent lessons provided. It was so user-friendly, easy to navigate, understand and brief. I will certainly refer this site on to others. Thanks again for all that has been put into this presentation. It is so appreciated."

> "I think your information and suggestions are (surprising to me) very good and insightful. Thank You Very Much! (I'm going to copy your web address so I can go back and refresh myself, as well as sending it to friends & family to give them insight to this disease and ways to help families."

> "I like the way the lessons are presented. They are clear, concise and helpful."

Outcomes from a qualitative study indicate widespread interest in implementing iGeriCare from the perspective of experts/clinicians involved in dementia care and care partner education.(Levinson, Ayers, et al., 2020) A wide range of stakeholders have adopted iGeriCare as part of their clinical workflows to date, 'prescribing' it to care partners, including: community physicians involved in dementia care, many regional Alzheimer Society educators, and community volunteer initiatives such as the Health TAPESTRY program.

5. The learning outcomes

In March 2021, we implemented the validated IAM4all survey for lessons. The IAM4all systematically documents reflection on health information, delivered or retrieved from electronic knowledge resources.(Pluye et al., 2014) It enhances reflective learning, evaluation of knowledge resources, and two-way knowledge exchange between information users and information providers.(Pluye *et al.*, 2014 Of 219 total responses, 95% completed the survey. Of the respondents, 45% were family care partners, 23% were concerned they may have mild cognitive impairment or dementia, and 10% were healthcare providers. In terms of impact, 93% found the lessons relevant or very relevant, and 99% of respondents felt they understood the information well or very well. There were a wide range of thoughts about the lessons: respondents felt the lessons taught them something new (55%), validated what they do or did (56%), reassured them (48%), refreshed their memory (39%), and motivated them to learn more (58%). 98% of respondents said that they would use the information from the lesson. Ways in which they would use the information included: better understand something (71%), do something (29%), do things differently (37%), and discuss with someone else (52%). Over 91% of respondents expected to benefit from using the information from the lesson, including: improve their health or well-being (48%), improve the health or well-being of the person they care for (46%), be less worried (44%), prevent a problem (31%), handle a problem or the worsening of a problem (48%), or decide something with someone else (28%).

At the end of the micro-learning campaign, we invite subscribers to do the Dementia Knowledge Assessment Tool, version 2 (DKAT2). The DKAT2 evaluates foundation-level knowledge dementia and care in family carers and care staff. It can help establish needs for, and outcomes of, education programs and informational resources in a feasible way, minimises burden, and facilitates comparisons across family and staff carer groups.(Toye *et al.*, 2014) Since September 2019, we have received 139 responses to the assessment, with a 96% completion rate. The average score is 77% (16/21), with a median score of 81%. The mean score is 10% better than typical population-based performance, which has an average score of 67% (14/21).(Toye *et al.*, 2014)

6. Plans to further develop the initiative

The iGeriCare initiative has also spawned other innovations, such as our educational prescription app for clinicians, email-based microlearning, and live online sessions.(Levinson, Bousfield, *et al.*, 2020) We received funding from the Canadian Institute for Health Research (CIHR) to translate and disseminate iGeriCare to francophone speaking audiences provincially and nationally in Canada. Peer-reviewed grant funding was also received to adapt iGeriCare for healthcare worker education. Recent peer-reviewed grant funding was obtained for a randomized clinical trial of the iGeriCare intervention to better quantify changes in knowledge, self-efficacy and burden among care partners of people living with dementia. Interest in the project is leading to other research collaborations, including expanding the content on iGeriCare to include material related to delirium, frailty, falls, and person-centred language. The award-winning project has also received regional, provincial, and national media coverage in Canada on CHCH television, CBC Radio, and CBC's The National. The initiative will also be featured in an upcoming report to the Canadian parliament on the national dementia strategy.

In summary, the iGeriCare platform is a readily scalable solution for clinician-prescribed care partner education to complement traditional approaches. It can potentially provide an efficient, effective, and cost-effective method to address important dementia care partner educational needs. This has implications at the level of both the healthcare system and the health of individual care partners.

References

Allen, M. and Sites, R. (2012) *Leaving ADDIE for SAM: An Agile Model for Developing the Best Learning Experiences*. American Society for Training and Development.

Canadian Academy of Health Sciences (2019) *Improving the quality of life and care of persons living with dementia and their caregivers*. Available at: https://cpp.178.myftpupload.com/wp-content/uploads/2019/04/REPORT.pdf.

Clark, R. C. and Mayer, R. E. (2016) *E-learning and the science of instruction*. 4th edn. Wiley.

Deeken, F. et al. (2019) 'Evaluation of technology-based interventions for informal caregivers of patients with dementia—A meta-analysis of randomized controlled trials', *American Journal of Geriatric Psychiatry*, 27(4), pp. 426–445. doi: 10.1016/j.jagp.2018.12.003.

Graham, C. et al. (2012) 'Overarching questions for patient surveys : development report for the Care Quality Commission (CQC)', *Oxford: The Picker Institute Europe*.

Health Quality Ontario (2018) *Recommendations for adoption: Dementia care in the community.*, *Queen's Printer for Ontario*. Available at: https://hqontario.ca/Portals/0/documents/evidence/quality-standards/qs-dementia-recommendations-for-adoption-en.pdf

Krug, S. (2013) *Don't Make Me Think, Revisitied: A Common Sense Approach to Web Usability*. 3rd edn. New Riders.

Levinson, A. J., Bousfield, J., et al. (2020) 'A Novel Educational Prescription Web-Based Application to Support Education for Caregivers of People Living With Dementia: Development and Usability Study With Clinicians.', *JMIR human factors*, 7(4), p. e23904. doi: 10.2196/23904.

Levinson, A. J., Ayers, S., et al. (2020) 'Barriers and Facilitators to Implementing Web-Based Dementia Caregiver Education From the Clinician's Perspective: Qualitative Study', *JMIR Aging*, 3(2), p. e21264. doi: 10.2196/21264.

NICE Satmetrix (no date) *What is Net Promoter*. Available at: https://www.netpromoter.com/know/

Ontario Ministry of Health and Long Term Care (2016) 'Developing Ontario's dementia strategy: A discussion paper', (September), pp. 1–54. Available at: https://files.ontario.ca/developing_ontarios_dementia_strategy_-_a_discussion_paper_2016-09-21.pdf.

Peterson, K. et al. (2016) 'In the information age, do dementia caregivers get the information they need? Semi-structured interviews to determine informal caregivers' education needs, barriers, and preferences', *BMC Geriatrics*, 16(1), p. 164. doi: 10.1186/s12877-016-0338-7.

Anthony J. Levinson, Stephanie Ayers, Lori Mosca, Alexandra Papaioannou, Sharon Marr and Richard Sztramko

Ploeg, J. et al. (2018) 'Caregiver-focused, web-based interventions: Systematic review and meta-analysis (Part 2)', *Journal of Medical Internet Research*, 20(10), p. e11247. doi: 10.2196/11247.

Pluye, P., Granikov V., et al. (2014) 'Development and Content Validation of the Information Assessment Method for Patients and Consumers', *JMIR Res Protoc*, 3(1), p. e7. doi: 10.2196/resprot.2908

Public Health Agency of Canada (2019) *A dementia strategy for canada: together we aspire*. Ottawa, Ontario. Available at: https://www.canada.ca/content/dam/phac-aspc/images/services/publications/diseases-conditions/dementia-strategy/National Dementia Strategy_ENG.pdf.

Ringer, T. J. et al. (2020) 'Understanding the educational and support needs of informal care-givers of people with dementia attending an outpatient geriatric assessment clinic', *Ageing and Society*. Cambridge University Press, 40(1), pp. 205–228. doi: 10.1017/S0144686X18000971.

Seffah, A. et al. (2006) 'Usability Measurement and Metrics: A Consolidated Model'. *Software Quality Journal*, 14(2), p. 159-178.

Sherifali, D. et al. (2018) 'Impact of internet-based interventions on caregiver mental health: Systematic review and meta-analysis', *Journal of Medical Internet Research*, 20(7), p. e10668. doi: 10.2196/10668.

Toye, C. et al. (2014) 'Dementia Knowledge Assessment Tool Version Two: Development of a tool to inform preparation for care planning and delivery in families and care staff', *Dementia*, 13(2), p. 248–256. doi: 10.1177/1471301212471960.

Ware, J.E. Jr, and Sherbourne, C.D. (1992) 'The MOS 36-Item Short-Form Health Survey (SF-36). I. Conceptual Framework and Item Selection', *Medical Care*, 30(6), p. 473-483.

Zarit, S.H., Reever, K.E., Back-Peterson, J. (1980) 'Relative of the Impaired Elderly: Correlates of Feelings of Burden', *The Gerontologist*, 20, p. 649-655.

Zhao, Y. et al. (2019) 'Web-based interventions to improve mental health in home caregivers of people with dementia: Meta-analysis', *Journal of Medical Internet Research*, 21(5), p. e13415. doi: 10.2196/13415.

Author biographies

Dr. Anthony Levinson is a psychiatrist, Director of the Division of e-Learning Innovation and John R. Evans Chair in Health Sciences Educational Research and Instructional Development at McMaster University. He maintains an active clinical practice in consultation-liaison psychiatry, specializing in complex neuropsychiatric disorders and mental health issues among the medically ill.

Stephanie Ayers is the Research Coordinator at the Division of e-Learning Innovation at McMaster University. She provides support to a number of research projects, assists with the development and submission of grant applications, and content creation.

Lori Mosca is the Lead, Special Projects at the Division of e-Learning Innovation at McMaster University. She has over 30 years of business experience including project management, data analysis, and e-learning development.

Dr. Alexandra Papaioannou is a Professor of Medicine at McMaster University, a Geriatric Medicine Specialist at Hamilton Health Sciences and Executive Scientific Director of the GERAS Centre for Aging Research. She holds an Eli Lilly Research Chair at McMaster University and is the past Director of the Division of Geriatric Medicine.

Dr. Sharon Marr is an Associate Professor at McMaster University, the Chair of the Regional Geriatric Program central (RGPc), Chair of the Division of Geriatric Medicine, and Chair of the Evaluations MD Undergrad Program. Her primary academic activities include teaching, education and administration at all levels from medical school through residency.

Dr. Richard Sztramko is an Assistant Professor at McMaster University. He practices both Geriatrics and General Internal Medicine at St. Peter's, Hamilton General, and Juravinski Hospitals. He focuses on eHealth interventions related to patient education, physician and healthcare provider communication, and home health monitoring.

OERu: Learning in a Digital Age

Rory McGreal[1] and Wayne Mackintosh[2]

[1]Athabasca University, Canada
[2]Otago Polytechnic, New Zealand
rory@athabascau.ca
wayne@oerfoundation.org

1. Introduction

The Open Education Resource Foundation (OERF), based in New Zealand, is an "independent, not-for-profit organisation that provides international networking and support for educational institutions, educators and learners to achieve their strategic objectives through Open Education". It is an active participant in the UNESCO OER Dynamic Coalition, hosts the WikiEducator community, co-ordinates the New Zealand Centre for Open Education Practice, and hosts New Zealand's UNESCO Chair in OER, which includes a commitment to UNESCO Sustainable Development Goal 4: Education for all.

The Foundation leads the implementation of the OER universitas (OERu), an international network of over 40 like-minded partner institutions (21 in developing countries) across five continents. The OERu Outreach Partnership Programme supports institutions in the developing world by providing free membership. The participating partners collaborate to assemble freely accessible, high quality, accredited online courses using open educational resources (OER) designed for independent study. OER consist of learning materials that have been released under an open intellectual property license, permitting their free use, adaptation, or re-purposing by others.

The OERu network of institutions offers free online courses for students worldwide. The OERu partners also provide affordable ways for learners to gain academic credit towards qualifications from recognised institutions by providing assessment-only services. The OERu network continually works towards widening access and reducing the cost of tertiary study for learners everywhere, and especially for those who are excluded from the formal education sector, particularly for those in developing countries. The operational cost of institution-based OERu assessment services are covered on a cost-recovery basis (or alternative revenue sources) providing pathways for students to achieve credible credentials for approved courses based solely on open education resources (OER).

OERu has the following core values:

- Free learning opportunities for all students worldwide.
- Affordable assessment services towards credible credentials.
- Open-source planning processes, technology and learning materials.
- Strategic philanthropy.
- Sustainable education futures.

1.1 Learning in a Digital Age Micro-courses

The OERu course site hosts an innovative, capacity-building package of micro-courses *Learning in a Digital Age (LiDA)*. The underpinning pedagogy includes embracing active learning and open educational practices, which itself is designed to promote innovation using digital literacy skills and OER capacity, by offering learners both a pathway towards independent learning through the internet, and encouragement to create their own openly licensed digital media.

The LIDA course development constitutes a component of a number of significant milestones within the global OER movement. It is the world's first OER-based programme implementing transnational micro-credentialing, with pathways to achieving formal academic course credit towards university-level qualifications in four countries. The LiDA micro-credential comprising four micro-courses has been evaluated for equivalency the New Zealand Qualifications Authority on the New Zealand Qualifications Framework. Using bilateral articulation agreements, LiDA is approved for credit transfer at OERu partner institutions in the USA, Canada and the United Kingdom. The OERu network hosts the world's first university-level exit qualification in the United Kingdom, that is based entirely on OER open online courses. LIDA qualifies for transcript credit towards the *Certificate of Higher Education Business (OERu)* conferred by the University of the Highlands and Islands in Scotland as well as the *Certificate of General Studies*, conferred by Thompson Rivers University in Canada.

2. The infrastructure

Our key learning at the OER Foundation has been to design for re-use as a principal point of departure, using Free and Open-Source Software (FOSS) technologies underpinned by open, transparent and collaborative planning approaches. While this combination of radical openness is not necessarily the path of "least resistance" in the short term, it enables iterative but agile responses for building and sharing open education solutions for the benefit of many organisations in a sustainable way.

Intentionally, the Foundation does not use a learning management system for delivery of courses. Rather, we develop content collaboratively in an open wiki which provides detailed version control for multiple remix scenarios. A collection of wiki pages constituting a micro-course are published to WordPress - an open-source content management system – thus enabling any institution to host their own instances of OERu courses at minimal cost. We have developed a component-based ecosystem comprising "best of breed" FOSS interaction technologies (forums, social media, annotation, commenting etc.) with open solutions to aggregate mentions from these distributed technologies into a single course feed. The learner discussions are hosted on the FOSS application *Discourse*. However, the discussion interactions from different sites located around the world are being aggregated into a "Twitter-like" feed of learner mentions. This provides a powerful example of a unique global collaboration that would be difficult to replicate using closed solutions.

2.1 Technical infrastructure

OERu, adhering to their "open" principles, has created an open source "Next Generation Digital Learning Environment" (NGDLE) to meet the needs of learners, consortium partners, and OER collaborators. The NGDLE is an example of a global computing infrastructure. It is a distributed, loosely coupled component model, consisting entirely of open-source applications. All OERu services are hosted on this open technology infrastructure. This approach has significant advantages which can enhance the quality of digital services used in education, while vastly reducing costs. This NDGLE can also increase the autonomy and resilience of technical solutions while providing unprecedented technology-related learning opportunities and agency for learners and educators alike.

The NGDLE infrastructure currently consists of four separate nodes, supporting OERu activities, located in the USA, Germany, Australia and New Zealand. All of these servers run the open-source operating system, Linux. Because OERu runs Linux on all servers, there is no cost involved for the operating system. We can run as many or as few systems as we want at a fixed cost. Only the sunk cost of the technologist's time and the relative computing resource requirements are variable. In addition, the network houses multiple services in *Docker* containers. "*We6*" (WikiEducator) is the original OERu server, and it runs the *Mediawiki* technology on which our first initiative was built. *Rocket.Chat* is used for synchronous real-time communications, including text & media messages, audio and video calls with OERu personnel, and with the broader partner and learner community. *Matomo* (formerly *Piwik*) allows OERu staff to track the use of websites. This application is functionally similar to Google Analytics, but with the advantage or maintaining privacy. No information is released to Google or any others. We host an instance of *BigBlueButton* for web-conferencing and *Mastodon* as a federated social media site for learners. Other services, include *YourLS*, a link shortener and *Semantic Scuttle*, a social bookmarking application, as well as several test systems including replicas of websites. The applications chosen as components are all the products of different communities, different developers, and different technologies. Nevertheless, all components adhere to a set of well tested robust and scalable internet software service patterns. Moreover, as a result of this commitment to open source, the annual infrastructure costs, of this eminently scalable network using four servers is less than USD8500.

2.2   Pedagogical infrastructure

OERu micro-courses are designed for independent study (as a small non-profit organisation, the OER Foundation does not have the financial resources to provide tutor support). However, the design is underpinned by Anderson's Interaction Equivalency Theorem, by providing robust student-content interaction and designing our courses for high-levels of peer learning support. The courses are also informed by Holmberg's theory of guided didactic conversion using simulated lecturer-student conversations, which are embedded in the course materials. To support this, OERu has created a dedicated student support site which provides help, including screen cast videos on how to study using the OERu online platform.

Using the NGDLE, learner interactions are distributed across the web using "best of breed" open-source technologies. These distributed interactions are aggregated into a live course feed. LiDA micro-courses are designed to build capability for participants to learn on the internet rather than learning in a classroom or via a single software application like a learning management system. These micro-courses incorporate a wide range of media, including video signposts for each learning pathway, while at the same time ensuring that learners can succeed in the course without watching the videos, due to cost of bandwidth in many parts of the developing world. Interactive content has been embedded into the courses, providing a wide variety of different activities (readings, case studies, reflections, course comments, discussion forums, social media posts etc.), and interactive quizzes with immediate feedback on correct and incorrect answers. A key feature in the courses is the adoption of a pedagogy of discovery where learners identify, evaluate and share open access resources in pursuit of their own learning interests for designated activities.

The LIDA course package is focused on building capability for online learning and associated digital

literacies in context. Relevant digital skills are embedded in context, so for example, learners can master how to annotate webpages using *hypothes.is,* while researching the differences in digital skills versus digital literacies. Moreover, learners can opt-in to receive course instructions for each session via email. These personalised email communications are automated using the open source *Mautic* marketing automation software hosted by the OER foundation. Our data shows improved learner retention when course instructions are sent via email. The OERu also provides a dedicated social media site (mastodon.oeru.org) and support forums for all its courses (forums.oeru.org). Learners help their peers and frequently volunteers from the open academic community offer support to learners.

The OER Foundation's long-standing commitment to openness in all its forms has secured a pathway for context-specific adoption and adaptation. Meanwhile, the process of refining and adapting courses, both pedagogically and technically, itself continues to develop the capacity, and the passion, of the individuals and institutions involved.

3. The challenges

The origin of LiDA was a short course entitled "Open Content Licensing for Educators" (OCL4Ed) developed collaboratively with funding support from the UNESCO Office for the Pacific States in 2011. OCL4Ed was originally developed as wiki-based course to support collaborative authoring enabled by the version control of the Mediawiki software environment. However, several shortcomings in course delivery were discovered in the initial iteration of the course. Many learners were not familiar with navigating wiki-based courses. Replicating the course for re-use by different institutions was cumbersome. In addition, initially, there were no assessment or credential options for formal academic credit. Moreover, as a standalone micro-course equating to 40 notional learning hours, the first micro-courses were not of sufficient scope to qualify for full course credit.

In 2015, the OERu international network therefore commenced development of the *Learning in a Digital Age* (LiDA) online course, encompassing OCL4Ed and other aspects of digital literacy required for 21st century innovation, learning and teaching. An international network of experts and professional educators worked together to investigate course outlines from similar university courses and identify the foundational requirements for the LiDA curriculum. This included an open crowdsourcing activity inviting educators to submit comments and concepts for inclusion. This work resulted in the creation of a collection of four openly licensed micro-courses:

1. Digital literacies for online learning (LiDA101)
2. Digital Citizenship (LiDA102)
3. Open education, copyright and open licensing in a digital world (LiDA103 and the successor to OCDL4Ed)

4. Critical media literacies and associated digital skills (LiDA104).

We developed scripting solutions to publish a collection of wiki pages constituting a course to publish a "snapshot" of the materials to the WordPress content management system. This solution has enabled version control for collaborative authoring, while providing the ability for any institution to host their own instances of responsive open online courses for learners studying using mobile devices. This technical approach has facilitated remix and reuse of OERu courses. For example, North West University in South Africa remixed sections from the OERu's *Introduction to Entrepreneurship* series of micro-courses to offer a customised micro-course for inclusion in their Introduction to Business Management (BMAN111) course. Students were required to work through this micro-course hosted by OERu and complete a series of quizzes which contributed towards their continuous assessment mark for the course.

4. How the initiative was received

LiDA micro-courses have been offered to more than 7,800 learners from over 90 different countries as of May 2021. Their ages range from 18 to 68 years and nearly half the learners were not native-English speakers, of which 64% were female and 66% were in full-time paid employment. The majority (50%) of learners indicated that their primary purpose for participating was for professional development, while 17% each indicated reskilling for a new career or for personal development as their main motivation.

The OERu administers an optional OERu new participant survey where we collect demographic information and data on learner experiences with online learning, and their reasons for studying with OERu. This helps them to not only progress but also to inform the design of the courses and support the development of future courses. So, there is an online course evaluation survey for each micro-course to review effectiveness of the design. Staff also monitor anonymous website analytics to evaluate how OERu course sites are utilised by learners, consistent with the privacy requirements of the European General Data Protection Regulation.

The OERu encourages learners to publish the outputs of their learning activities using personal blog sites, supporting the development of digital literacies but more importantly, providing learners control over the innovations they produce even after the course has finished, Feedback from course evaluations and server data have indicated that learners were having difficulty in identifying and registering the correct url for the RSS feed page of their individual course blogs. This is important because it is used for integrating blog posts into the live course feed (RSS is a standardised system for distributing machine readable content on the Internet). Staff addressed this challenge by developing new open-source software code to automatically detect the blog feed url for OERu learners and registering this for harvesting on the course site.

5. The learning outcomes

OERu has established a working model for transnational micro-credentialling for approved university qualifications. Assessment of outcomes for the LiDA courses are purposefully designed as building blocks to motivate and establish confidence for success before learners attempt the optional summative assessment for micro-credentials with pathways to achieving official academic course credit. Each micro-course has a basic knowledge test covering core concepts. Learners who pass the knowledge test can earn a Digital Badge for Participation for free (or purchase the PDF Certificate of Participation for a nominal fee of NZ$10)- These objective assessments are formative and do not qualify for credit. Feedback on correct and incorrect answers are provided for learners. Skill challenges at the end of each learning pathway constitute sub-components of the final summative assessment. Learners gain the opportunity to practice their skills by applying their learning while receiving feedback from their peers before revising and preparing submissions for the final assessment. All summative assessments for the associated micro-credentials for the micro-courses, are subject to an independent pre-assessment moderation to ensure alignment with the learning outcomes. Rubrics are published on the course sites for each summative assessment providing detail on the performance criteria. Learners who successfully complete the micro-credentials can qualify for credit towards university-level qualifications in Canada, New Zealand, UK and the United States. Moreover, published as OER, any institution can reuse the LiDA assessments for credit recognition towards locally approved qualifications without incurring course design or development costs.

As assessments for formal credit are conducted by individual OERu partners, due to privacy restrictions the OERF does not have access to performance metrics of individual learners completing courses for formal credit. However, the course evaluation survey provides some insight. 95% Of learners agree that they were generally satisfied with their learning experience, with 85% of learners indicating that they would personally recommend the course to others. There is evidence of positive learning. Prior to commencing the course, 20% of learners rated their knowledge of OER as "Sufficient" with only 15% rating their knowledge as "Excellent". After taking the course, self-evaluation of knowledge had improved with 45% of learners rating their knowledge as "Sufficient" and 36% of learners rating their knowledge as "Excellent".

6. Plans to further develop the initiative

The OER Foundation is presently collaborating with UNESCO and the ICDE, who are leading a consultation for developing a culturally appropriate French instance of the LiDA micro-course on Open Education, Copyright and Open Licensing, in partnership with the French Ministry of Education, the French Thematic University, and the virtual universities of Francophone Africa. On conclusion of this consultation, the course will be published on the OERu open technology infrastructure for re-use by any institution. In addition, we are currently collaborating with OEGlobal to host an instance of this same micro-course on OEGlobal's own course site.

The implementation of the OERu strongly suggests that the status quo for IT infrastructure in higher education institutions is neither the only way to do things, nor is it the best way. Because the OERu is unbound by historical decisions or conventions, it is able to pioneer new approaches, from an "educational technology expert" perspective. OERu is driven by open principles and very tight resource constraints, but only need fulfil the vision: to build a rich, fit-for-purpose infrastructure for learners and OER collaborators alike, which has the potential to scale to facilitate large numbers of global learners, effectively addressing the UNESCO SDG4: Education for all. Implementing an open-source end-to-end service gives the OERu a unique perspective and experience compared to organisations who only implement the occasional open-source component in the midst of IT infrastructure dominated by commercial software that is costly and extremely restrictive by comparison. OERu is building (anonymous) monitoring systems into these services to ensure that evidence of success and failure can be collected and measured (without impinging on the privacy of learners or collaborators). The insights gained will be openly shared.

Author biographies

Wayne Mackintosh is founding director of the OER Foundation headquartered at Otago Polytechnic, New Zealand. He is coordinating the establishment of the OERu, an international innovation partnership which aims to widen access to more affordable education for all. Wayne holds the UNESCO/ICDE Chair in OER at Otago Polytechnic and serves as a member of the Board of Directors of the OER Foundation.

Rory McGreal is Professor in the master's in integrated studies programme at Athabasca University, Alberta Canada. He is also the UNESCO/International Council for Open and Distance Education Chair in Open Educational Resources and Director of the Technology Enhanced Knowledge Research Institute (TEKRI).

An Online PhD Programme in Computer Science and Information Technology

Izzeldin Mohamed Osmasn
Sudan University of Science and Technology
izzeldin@acm.org

Abstract: This initiative is a blended learning Internet mediated PhD programme in Computer Science and Information Technology run by Sudan University of Science and Technology (SUST). It brings together PhD supervisors from renowned universities worldwide. They come to SUST to meet the students and present their research areas. The students take online courses with their selected professors and supervisors. The students reside in Sudan and the neighboring countries (Ethiopia, Egypt, Nigeria and Gulf countries). Each student must have access to the Internet. Online meeting software has been used on laptops and mobile phones to provide online access including student presentations and discussions. Examinations and progress seminars are conducted face to face at SUST. After COVID19 progress seminars are conducted online. Competent technicians manage the system and schedule sessions and meetings which is challenging as the participants could be from different time zones extending from America, UK, Europe and all the way to Australia. Another challenge was the intermittent irregularities of the Internet in some locations (such as Gondor in Ethiopia). Full recording of the sessions was made available for the students to catch up with missing sessions. This Programme is now in its eleventh year. Over two hundred research papers were published. Fifty-three women and fifty-one men have already graduated and most of them have been promoted to the status of assistant professors in their universities. Two women and two men graduates are now deans of colleges. A panel of external and internal examiners assesses the progress of each student and continuously evaluates the Programme and raises suggestions for corrective actions. Plans have already started to enable graduates to pursue post-doctoral research at SUST in cooperation with professors from the developed countries. A project with a French university involving four graduates has started. It is planned to seek financial assistance to adequately support and sustain the Programme.

1. Introduction

The PhD degree is a mandatory requirement for promotion in academia. Many African countries have problems with offering serious PhD programmes in Computers Science and Information Technology because they suffer from a severe brain drain which has led to a scarcity of qualified PhD supervisors. It is not easy, for lecturers (holding master's degrees) at local universities, to find PhD programmes. Only few fortunate ones manage to travel abroad to be enrolled in foreign PhD programmes. For women, the difficulty to pursue education abroad is very high due to economic, social and family commitments in Sudan and many African countries. This Programme is located in Sudan. It is in the field of Computer Science and Information Technology but could be replicated in other fields at any other place with similar difficulties.

Sudan has 34 public universities, eight private universities and over fifty private colleges (Ministry of Higher Education 2021). Each of these higher education institutions has at least one kind of computer studies bachelor programme. The Sudanese Ministry of Higher Education requires each academic programme to have at least one staff member qualified at PhD level. Many of the colleges fall short of satisfying this requirement due to the scarcity of PhD holders in this specialization which is exacerbated by the temptation to work abroad and enjoy the lucrative salaries in the neighbouring oil-rich countries. This Programme attempts to provide the required qualified personnel that would assist higher education institutions in mitigating this problem. This Programme employs ICT to enable students to pursue their studies and to have their research supervised by knowledgeable and experienced professors from renowned universities worldwide. The first batch of students was admitted in 2010. A student in the Programme can attend lectures, receive supervision, present seminars, lead discussions and interventions using her/his personal computer or laptop at home or office in his hometown. She/He only needs to come to the university at the end of the semester to take exams face to face, meet a supervisor and give presentations or progress seminars. Later during the COVID19 precautions most of the presentations and the seminars were conducted online.

1.1   Objectives

This initiative is a blended learning programme which employs the Internet to benefit from the worldwide resources in order to fulfill the following objectives:

- To qualify lecturers at local universities to obtain a PhD in Computer and Information Technology from SUST in current research topics under qualified professors at an affordable cost
- To empower women in academia by providing the opportunity to obtain the necessary qualification (Munoz-Hermandez & Osman 2016).
- To assist in providing qualified PhD holders needed by Higher Education.

This Programme seeks to fulfill these objectives by qualifying students in the most recent and current areas in this rapidly changing technology using blended learning: face to face and Internet mediated online learning. Currently the Programme is in its eleventh year.

1.2   The Operation of the Programme

A new batch of about forty qualified students is selected and admitted to the Programme each year. Each year nine professors from renowned universities are selected from those who answer the Call for Supervisors issued by SUST. They meet the new batch of students in Khartoum for a whole week where each professor presents his research area and answers the questions of the students and discusses the possible research topics with those who are interested in his research area. Then each student picks two areas (two professors/ two possible supervisors) and studies an introductory course with the professor through weekly online lectures and meetings. On passing the exams on the two courses, each student chooses one research area (i.e one supervisor) for his/her PhD research. The student then prepares his research proposal under the guidance of his supervisor. The research proposals are presented in Khartoum in the presence of the supervisor and an assigned examination panel. Each supervisor meets his students periodically online. Each student conducts an annual progress seminar at SUST attended by his supervisor and the examination panel. This process continues until the student finishes his research and presents his thesis for the final PhD examination.

2. Infrastructure

The infrastructure consists of the students, the professors, the technology and the administration.

2.1 The students

The students are college and university lecturers and teaching assistants who satisfy the admission requirements for the PhD Programme in the broad field of computer studies (Information Technology, Computer Science, Software Engineering, etc.). They can afford to devote about thirty hours per week throughout the period of their full-time registration and one month full-time at the university (SUST) during their summer vacation for the face-to-face activities (examinations, lectures, group activities and meeting their supervisors). The students are from Sudan and the neighbouring countries. Table 1 shows the total numbers of all students who joined the Programme. Already a hundred and four students have graduated with PhD in Computer Science and Information Technology and about twenty students have dropped out.

An annual progress seminar has to be presented by the student. It is judged by a panel consisting of the supervisor, an internal and an external examiner. A bi-annual progress report describing the performance of each student would be submitted through the Programme Coordinator to SUST.

Table 1: Distribution of students by country

	Male	Female
Sudan	120	99
Sudanese in the Gulf Region	19	50
Ethiopia	10	
Jordon		1
Bahrain		1
UAE	1	
Egypt	1	1
Chad	1	
Nigeria	1	
Total	**153**	**152**

2.2 Professors

Professors are selected from those who answer the Call for Supervisors issued every year by the Programme. They are from universities all over the world (see Table 2).

Table 2: Distribution of participating professors by country

Country	No of professors	Country	No of professors
Australia	1	Malaysia	3
Brazil	1	Morocco	1
Canada	6	Poland	1
Czech	1	Portugal	1
Denmark	1	South Africa	5
Egypt	4	Spain	2
France	3	Sudan	3
Germany	2	Sweden	1
Ireland	1	Tunis	1
Italy	3	Turkey	1
Japan	1	UK	4
Jordon	1	USA	4
Total			52

On their first meeting with the new incoming batch of students, the professors (prospective supervisors) give seminars explaining their areas of expertise and the possible research opportunities. The professors then teach introductory courses in their own research areas online. The students choose two professors and attend two introductory courses online. After passing the two courses, each student chooses one professor to act as his supervisor for the research portion of his PhD. Each professor supervises 4-5 students. He guides the group through his own research area. His contact with the group is through scheduled meetings using the Internet (Cisco Webex 2021) and at least one face-to-face meeting coordinated by SUST in Khartoum around August each year. The supervisor follows his students for a period of 3 to 4 years until graduation. Normally students graduate at different times depending on their competency and individual circumstances.

2.3   The Technology

Cisco WebEx software has been used by the Programme since 2012. Cisco's WebEx facility provides a virtual space for people to meet online with video conferencing, sharing documents, sharing desktops, sharing a whiteboard, participating in text based private and group chats, and recording a meeting. Cisco WebEx provides both a desktop implementation and a mobile implementation (Cisco Webex 2021). Competent technicians operate, support and schedule the service. The Dropbox application (Dropbox Inc. 2018) is used for storing and sharing material including files, videos and photos. The relevant facilities available on the Internet are also employed and in particular social media for students own discussions.

SUST developed an application to enhance the performance of the system. It alerts the operator to take appropriate actions such as shutting down cameras or unused microphones. Another application assists the operator in scheduling sessions bearing in mind the different time zones and the choices of the supervisors and the students.

SUST has benefited from its previous experience in employing the Internet in education (Cronje 2006) and from the contributions of the supervisors in customizing the technology to overcome local constraints (Butgereit & Osman 2014). Some innovative educational online teaching techniques were experimented (Butgereit 2015).

2.4   Administration

The Programme is managed by Coordinators from SUST. Each batch of students has a Coordinator who is in close contact with students. He coordinates between the students, the supervisors, SUST Graduate College and the departments in charge of logistics.

3. The Challenges

The Programme was confronted by many challenges in its first years which were overcome in different innovative ways. These challenges were as follows:

1. The bandwidth required by the meetings' management software to provide text, audio and live video simultaneously is higher than the bandwidth available to many students and that affected the quality of the service. This was resolved by closing the student cameras so that in a conversation no photos of the speakers were transmitted. The microphones were open only when a student is speaking or once he opts to participate in a discussion. The professor or the student delivering the seminar distributes the opportunities for interventions.
2. The Internet service in some locations is not reliable (e.g Gondar, Ethiopia) and in some rural areas the bandwidth occasionally drops leading to some disruption of the service. This was resolved by having full recording of all sessions including presentations and discussions. A student can always go back and play the recording of any session.
3. The scheduling of sessions was a challenging problem in the beginning. A session has to be scheduled at a time convenient for the professor and for his students. The participants are normally in different time zones. The professor could be in Canada or Australia and the students in Sudan and Bahrain. By judiciously drafting the time slots and the patient consultation of professors and groups of students, the competent manager of the schedule (Miss Sarah Mohamed) has consistently published schedules acceptable by the students and the professors. The schedule could contain meetings between 7 am to 10 pm Khartoum time (GMT + 2) Saturday to Thursday, benefiting from the situation that professors and students could participate in a meeting while they are at home.
4. During the last three years the exchange rate of the Sudanese Pound (SDG) against the USD dropped sharply. This was a real challenge because the fees of the local students are paid in SDG while the professors are paid in USD. The resulting deficit was partly covered by SUST and partly by raising the student fees. In addition, the Programme administration has been actively seeking donations from local donors. The drop in the exchange rate became so huge in 2021 that no new batch of students was admitted.
5. The Programme has been designed to be a three-year PhD programme. However, it became evident that most of the students would require more than three years to graduate. Many students are employed part-time, and many women are devoting a significant portion of their time to their families. This phenomenon would extend the participation of the professor for the

given batch which would burden the budget of the Programme. To minimize this problem the students are required to pay additional fees for the semesters spent over the assumed three and a half years. Apparently, this has given positive results, but they have not been quantified yet.

4. The Response of Users and Participants

The Programme has made a very good reputation for itself. The number of applicants is increasing year after year. The students are happy with the Programme and they value the opportunity that it has given them. Examples of the responses of the students are expressed in a video, (see SUST Students Video 2017). Two Ethiopian universities (University of Gondar and University of Bahr Dar) have already signed agreements with SUST to annually sponsor some of their lecturers to join the Programme.

The participating professors have shown great interest in the Programme. Some professors have expressed their experience and positive interaction with the Programme in the form of published papers (Butgereit & Osman 2014, Butgereit 2015 and Munoz-Hermandez & Osman 2016). Many professors make extraordinary arrangements for their students for the online use of the resources of their universities and for hosting some of the students to conduct their research and experiments there. All professors whose students graduated informed the administratiors of the Programme of their interest to supervise another group of students. Some professors have been interested in forming exchange agreements with SUST. One such agreement will enable four graduates of the Programme to pursue post doctorate research at a French university. A similar agreement with a Spanish university is underway.

5. The Learning Outcomes

The students researched current topics covering a wide spectrum of Computer Science and Information Technology. They have published their research in journals and made presentations in local, regional and international conferences. Over 200 journal research papers were published and about 100 papers were published in the proceedings of conferences. Fifty-three women and fifty-one men have graduated from the Programme. Those working in academia in Sudan and abroad have been promoted to the status of assistant professor. Four graduates (two men and two women) are now deans of colleges of Computer and Information Technologies in two top public universities (SUST and University of Gezira) and two private universities (Ahfad University for Women and University of Garden City) (Brennan 2016). A bright example is SUST College of Computer Science and Information Technology which in 2014 had many women lecturers (holding Master's degree) but only one woman assistant professor (holding PhD) and now in 2021 it has 10 women assistant professors and 2 women associate professors accounting for 64% of academic staff of the College. Thus, the Programme has fully achieved all of its objectives. This is summarized in Table 4.

Table 4: Summary of the achievement of objectives

Objectives	Achievements, 2010 – 2021
To assist in providing qualified PhD holders needed by Higher Education	104 students graduated. 4 graduates assumed Deanships of universities. Example: SUST College of Computer Science and Information Technology (CCSIT): In 2021, of the 19 members of academic staff who have PhD, 13 are graduates of the Programme.
To empower women in academia by providing the opportunity to obtain the necessary qualification	53 women graduated. 2 women assumed Deanship of universities. Example: SUST CCSIT in 2021: The Dean is a woman (graduate of the Programme). Of the 19 members of academic staff who have PhD, 12 are women (63%) of whom 10 are assistant professors (graduates of the Programme) and 2 are associate professors. (Brennan 2016) (Munoz-Hermandez & Osman 2016).
To qualify lecturers at local universities to obtain a PhD in Computer and Information Technology from SUST in current research topics under qualified professors at an affordable cost	Competent experienced professors from renowned universities supervised the students. Each student published at least two research papers in specialized journals. The tuition fees for the local students are less than 10% of the average fees of universities abroad. Most of the local students are residing at home.

The success of the Programme has encouraged SUST to start an Internet mediated PhD programme in Engineering and some other universities to create deanships for e-learning many years before COVID19 compelled educational institutions to adopt online learning.

The evaluation of the Programme has been a continuous process. The administrators of the Programme receive bi-annual progress reports from the supervisors. The panel of examiners evaluates the progress of each student every year and reports to the administrators of the Programme. The Graduate College of SUST conducts annual progress evaluations of the of the Programme.

6. Future Plans

The Programme will seek financial support and resources to enable the students to present their research results in the specialized international conferences and to build relationships with researchers with similar research interests. It plans to expand the cooperation with Ethiopian universities to a regional cooperation of universities whereby African universities can employ the Internet in sharing teaching and research resources. The Programme can be developed into a regional capacity building and research hub by supporting the post doctorate training for the graduates and expanding the cooperation of professors from the developed and developing countries.

Acknowledgements

This paper describes an initiative which is the outcome of the accumulation of ideas and the experimentation of the staff of SUST College of Computer Science and Information Technology blended by the vast knowledge and experience of many professors and academics from universities all over the world. This is to acknowledge all of their contribution. However, within this limited space, the author has to explicitly acknowledge the cooperation and encouragement of the present and former leadership of SUST, Deans of the College and administrators of the Programme. Finally, a special word of thanks and gratitude to Sarah Mohamed and to Dr Laurie Butgereit for editing an earlier version of this paper.

References

Brennan, W 2016 'PhD programme empowers women in Sudan – A case study', University World News, 14 October 2016. https://www.universityworldnews.com/post Accessed 7 September 2021

Butgereit, L 2015, 'Gamifying a PhD Taught Module: A Journey to Phobos and Deimos', IST-Africa 2015 Conference Proceedings, Paul Cunningham and Miriam Cunningham (Eds), IIMC International Information Management Corporation, 2015, ISBN: 978-1-905824-50-2

Butgereit, L. & Osman, I 2014, 'Flipping" an Online PhD programme between Sudan and South Africa', ISTAfrica 2014 Conference Proceedings, Paul Cunningham and Miriam Cunningham (Eds), IIMC International Information Management Corporation, 2014, ISBN: 978-1-905824-43-4

Cisco WebEx 2021, http://www.webex.com. Accessed 21 April 2021.

Cronje, J. C 2006, 'Pretoria to Khartoum - How we taught an Internet-supported Masters' programme across national, religious, cultural and linguistic barriers'. Educational Technology & Society, 2006, 9 (1), 276288.

Dropbox, Inc, Moovly 2018. https://www.dropbox.com Accessed 20 July 2018
Ministry of Higher Education, Statistics 2016, http://www.mohe.gov.sd Accessed 5 September 2016.
MUNOZ-HERNANDEZ, S. & OSMAN, I 2016, 'Using a Productive Distance PhD Programme to Empower Women in Academia', IST-Africa 2016 Conference Proceedings Paul Cunningham and Miriam Cunningham (Eds) IIMC International Information Management Corporation, 2016 ISBN: 978-1-905824-54-0
SUST Students Video, 2017   https://youtu.be/329P6WrMha0 Accessed 6 September 2021

Author biography

Izzeldin Mohamed Osman is Professor Emeritus at Sudan University of Science and Technology (SUST). He was president of SUST, professor of computer science at California State University and University of Khartoum. He was active in the UNESCO Information for all Programme. Since 2003 he has been involved in Internet mediated educational and training programmes.

TechTeach in a fully online learning environment

Filipe Portela
University of Minho, Guimarães, Portugal
cfp@dsi.uminho.pt

Abstract: Teaching processes are changing, and a new normal is being created. Students are even more demanding, and professors need to follow technology's evolution to increase their engagement in the classroom. Higher education students recognise that introducing new tools and learning methods can improve teaching quality and increase their learning motivation. Having this concern in mind, a new and innovative paradigm using Gamification emerged. TechTeach explores trending concepts and tools to promote an interactive teaching environment, increase students' engagement, and provide the best learning environment. After the presential approach's success, a case study was used to prove this approach's functionality and relevance in a fully online learning environment. The results show that the efforts were tremendous but beneficial to all. After 15,224 Messages, 200,000 Sessions, 208 online hour classes, 11,173 Downloads, three rescues, and 21 cards, 98.15% of active students got approval, and 85% of the students approved the gamification system. Also, 96.53% of the students considered this unit equal to or better than the others. With TechTeach, a classroom is no longer a boring place; it is a place to learn and enjoy regardless of whether it is physical or not.

1. Introduction

E-learning plays a vital role in the learning transformation process. Learning environments are being converted into flexible spaces, and new teaching approaches and methods are emerging. This transformation brings new challenges to society, and all the "players" face several difficulties adapting to this new way of learning (e.g., without face contact). The numbers of distractions and different ways of obtaining knowledge are enormous. This adaptation is an ongoing learning process, where Professors need to find new methods to bring students to the class and increase their engagement. Personally, e-learning is much more than put a subject online – it is the creation of a global ecosystem where all the stakeholders can be engaged together, share knowledge/experiences, and potentiate learning.

This case study represents five years of work and research as a coordinator of Web Programming Classes. Since 2017, a yearly question was performed about the teaching method. Most students (86.22% of 399) admitted to preferring interactive over traditional classes. So, the student's feedback potentiated the development of a new teaching paradigm named TechTeach. It is a global approach that has evolved since the beginning and combines B-learning, Bring Your Own Device (BYOD), Flipped and Interactive Classes, Gamification, Soft-skills Development, active learning, Project-Based Learning (PBL) with Team Based-Learning (TBL).

The will of creating an interactive way of learning led me to develop new tools. ioEduc arose first as a teaching support web/mobile platform containing several features. Then, ioChat was added, turning ioEduc into a complete online teaching platform with rooms, sharing and communication features. It is a clear example of how information systems and new technologies can reengineer teaching processes and promote digital transformation. This new paradigm aims to increase student's engagement in a course unit (CUnit) by making it more attractive and interactive. The weekly implementation plan is shown in Figure 1. This figure makes it possible to understand the plan by week and observe the knowledge assessment moments: individual - three Mini-Test (MT1, MT2 and MT3) and group project: two Control Points (CP1 and CP2) with a final presentation (FA) of the work.

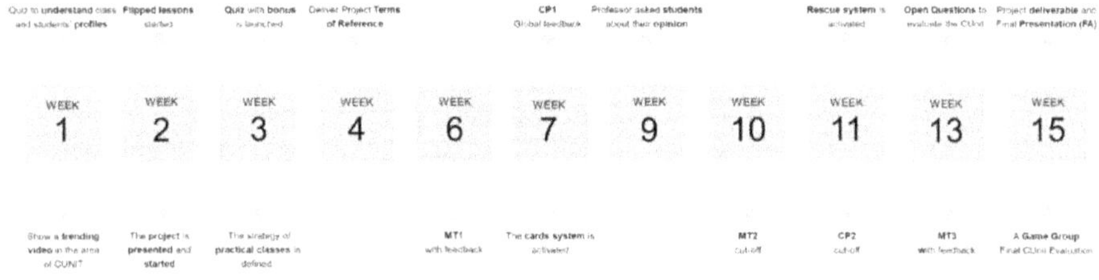

Figure 1 – TechTeach Weekly plan

We tested this approach in a fully online learning environment after the first experience in 2019/2020 (b-learning). In September 2020, the classes were moved to online mode, and several e-learning strategies were prepared to support the entire learning process. At the beginning of this process, two questions emerged to drive the study:

RQ1 - Is TechTeach ready or adapted to classes 100% online?

RQ2 - What is the effort needed? Is it worth it?

All the classes and assessment methods were conducted online, using sync and async activities. This experience was a challenge for everyone, and the results were promising. The proof of concept occurred on a subject with Ten European Credit Transfer and Accumulation System (ECTS) at the University of Minho with almost one hundred and seventy students. In the beginning, we defined two main goals according to the TechTeach paradigm:

- To Innovate and achieve the success of having a 100% Online CUnit (without issues).
- To use concepts like Gamification, PBL, Quizzes, Flipped Classes, and emerging tools to provide students with the best online learning environment possible (with an acceptance rate upper than 80%).

The working/teaching plan was based on the following assumptions:

- Full online classes (100%).
- Assess students' performance using Gamification mechanisms.
- Simulate the classroom environment through an online communication platform.
- Create dynamic, inclusive, and online assessments.
- Prepare learning content/tutorials to be carried out outside of classes (OT).
- Create an online repository (drive) with complementary information (books, articles, videos, or tutorials).
- Implement FAQs with the most common issues.
- Record the theoretical classes.
- Explore project-based learning with the application of a real case.
- Create rooms for doubts and online chat.
- Promote continuous assessment of the CUnit - direct contact with the class delegates.
- Explore the learning of soft skills (e.g., entrepreneurship, cross-learning, communication, adaptability, resilience, and leadership).

2. The infrastructure

TechTeach in an Online context (Figure 2) uses, essentially, Gamification, Flipped and Interactive Classrooms, Soft-skills, Project-Based Learning (PBL) and Team-Base Learning (TBL) to proportionate the best learning environment for the students.

This subsection does a brief overview of the approach infrastructure and tools used in this case study.

2.1 People and Groups

This case study had six professors (one coordinator, four assistants and one tutor) and 163 students. The role of each one is presented in Figure 3. Professor was the manager of the class, and the students were the leading player.

7th International e-Learning Excellence Awards

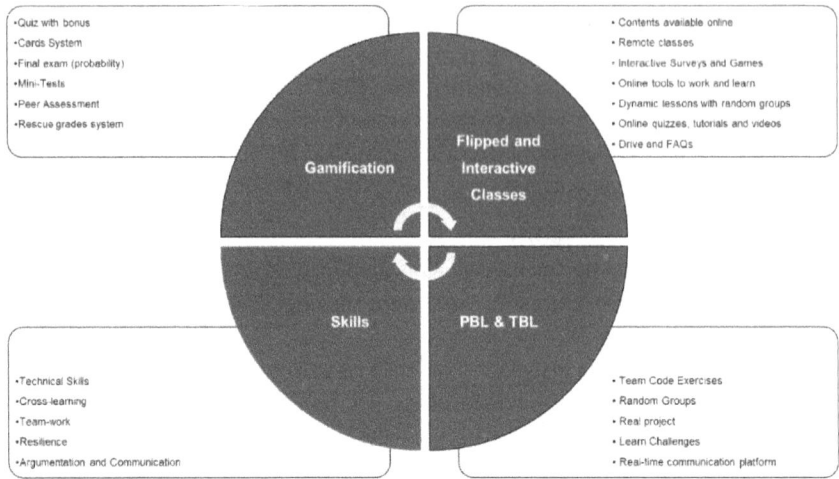

Figure 2 – TechTeach in the Online context

 Professor

"**referee** and **manager**" of the class ("game")

a. Promote **team learning** and **content research**;
b. Potentiate **project-based learning** with actual problems;
c. Promote exercises comprising the learning of **soft skills**;
d. Create a list of Frequently Asked Questions (**FAQs**);
e. Prepare the **communication system** and create all the rooms;
f. Create a weekly **quiz** to assess the students' knowledge;
g. Implement a **bonus** system to motivate the **participation**;
h. Create an **online drive** with tutorials, presentations, videos, documents, books, practical examples and other essential contents;
i. Promote a continuous **evaluation** of the **subject** and show that the students' opinion is relevant;
j. Implement and define the rules of the **rescue system**;
k. Create **interactive** and synchronized **assessment methods**;
l. Create **Kahoots** and **games** able to promote interactive discussion inside of the classroom.

 Student

leading "**player**"

a. Create an **account** on the e-Learning platform
b. **Study** the topics before the lesson;
c. **Explore** and learn new concepts;
d. **Participate** in the "**game**" - interacting with the environment and train their soft skills;
e. Ask for **recognition** or **rescue**;
f. Contribute to the **cross-learning**;
g. Contribute to the **improvement** and **evaluation** of the CUnit;
h. Be **active** in the **communication** platform;
i. Do not miss the **assessment tasks**;
j. Propose a **solution** to the project;
k. **Win points** to achieve better grade possible;
l. Do a Peer and Team **evaluation** of the **work**.

Figure 3 – TechTeach Rules adapted from (Portela, 2020)

The idea of creating a natural environment of coworking is also a concern of TechTeach. So, a project using a different work environment capable of mixing students' duties was prepared to proportionate a real/professional working experience. The students were divided into eight teams (+/-20 students) and 27 groups (+/-6 students).

This project ran in LP and TP classes. An LP class was composed of three groups where both groups were part of the same team. Each team worked together at TP classes;

however, the division was not performed by the group but by project roles. It represents a mix of people between LP and TP classes and allows knowledge sharing. Besides that, the team, groups, and areas also have a leader. Both had to do a weekly analysis of the work and show it to the professor.

Figure 4 shows an overview of the LP and TP classes distribution. TP classes were split into three different spaces - one being reserved to full-stacks, another to front-end developers and another to back-end developers - where teams worked, distributed by project role, and LP classes were organised by group. ioChat supported the entire workflow.

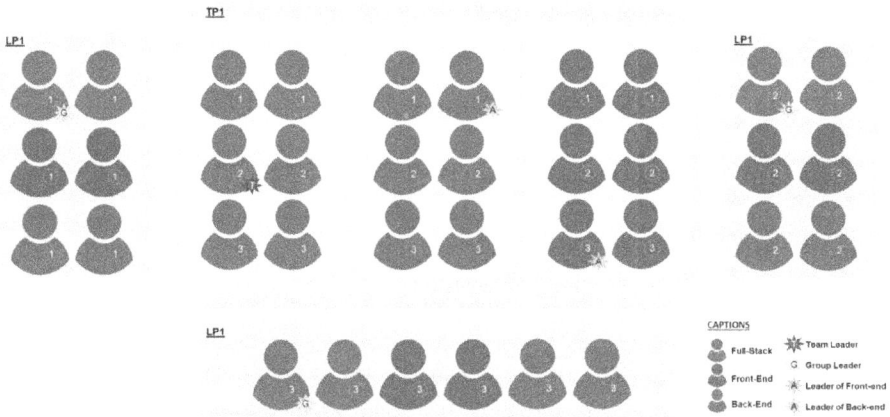

Figure 4 – Team Classes distribution (Portela, 2020)

1.2 Assessment mechanisms

This subject had a transversal and continuous assessment process to evaluate students, professors, and subjects. This CUnit has three assessment typologies:

- **Participation** - A weekly quiz with a bonus to award motivation, work, and engagement.
- **Project** – A real problem with peer assessment to evaluate individual effort and cards to value students' skills.
- **Mini-tests** - Three synchronised exercises to assess different parts of knowledge (Front-end, Back-end and Full-stack).

As happened with the students, professors and CUnit were also evaluated. This assessment occurred in two moments (middle and end), was anonymous and assessed several factors like the professor's knowledge, teaching skills, subject plan, and classes.

Finally, students applied the peer assessment two times during the project (PC2&FA) to evaluate work results and member dedication/effort. Group grades ranged from 0 to 20. The individual evaluation had reference-grade N, ranging from -4 and 4. This method also had a checkbox to select the option "student did not work" and a text field to justify the assessment. All the student grades were privately and individually released in their account at ioEduc.

2.2 Classes

The classes were ministered online using eLearning platforms. Each student had a plan with six hours of contact, 2 hours from each class type: Theoretical (T), Theoretical Practice (TP) and Laboratory Practice (LP).

Complementing the working plan, each student had two tutorial hours and six hours of autonomous work. The "working rules" were presented to the students in the first class and disseminated in ioChat.

2.3 Gamification Systems

A narrative was designed for each assessment method, and students knew from the beginning what they had to do to achieve specific goals. Gamification was applied in several moments through the following exercises/contexts.

Mini-Tests (MT)

The MT1 and MT3 grades were calculated using a pondered metric based on the achieved points, technical issues, questions weight, and answering time according to the average time of respondents (3rd quartile).

MT2 worked as a cut-off and had two programming exercises. Exercise 1 with code gaps, where the students must complete it with their personal data, and exercise 2, where they must use their skills/knowledge to unlock exercise 2.2. In the end, students achieved one of three possible grades in MT2:

-1   Student does not know the basics and should reprove to this component - 0%.

0   Student knows the basics and can advance - 100%.

1   Student knows the basics and overcomes all the challenges (e.g., unlock the 2nd part of the exercise) and must advance - 110%.

The final grade of MT was achieved by the formula *avg(MT1,MT3)*MT2*.

Quiz with bonus

Professor promoted a quiz every week, and the students had the opportunity to double their results. Every T class, a bonus was raffled from 10 to 15 students. Only the class attendants were eligible, and no one student could be selected more than two times without all the students being selected at least once. In the end, the student with the most points (P) without a bonus (K) had a grade of 20.

All the students with grades (G+K) >= P also had 20. The remaining students had a relative grade regarding P → (G+K)/P. The goal of this exercise was to motivate and award students who could hit more questions.

Cards System

It is an interactive system where the professor can do a continuous assessment of a student's performance. This system has two types of evaluation: Positive (white and blue) or negative (yellow, orange, and red), as shown in Figure 5. If a student has a good performance, he can receive a white and then a blue card. On the opposite side, he can receive a yellow, then orange and finally a red card.

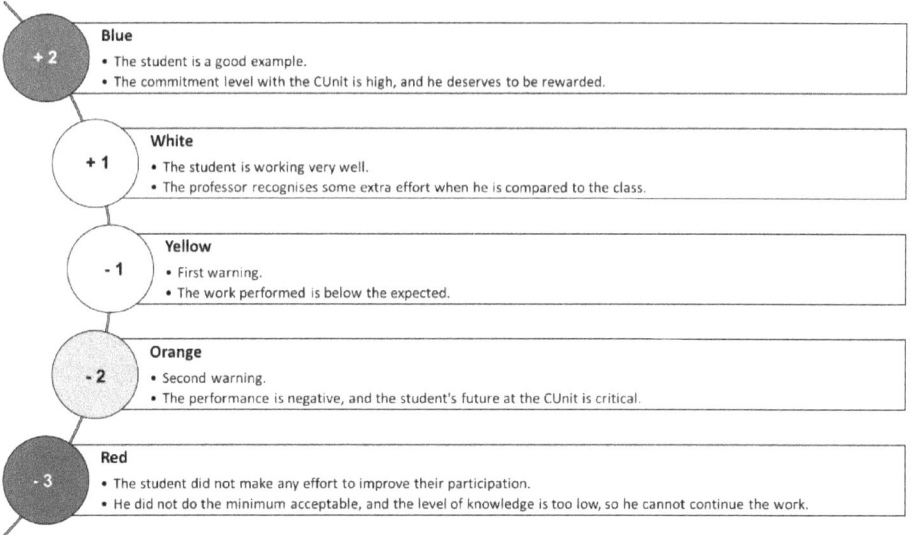

Figure 5 – Card's explanation

The card system was applied during the project, and the team leaders and professors attributed yellow (negative) or white cards (positive) to the students.

Rescue System

TechTeach gives the possibility for students to rescue a grade and have second chances to show their value. Each student can use this system only one time during the CUnit.

This possibility is available to anyone who has a negative grade and considers their degree unfair. After the student asks for redemption, the professor will analyse the request, and in case of being approved, he can continue their work as usual.

This system was available in MT2 to the students who had a -1 grade. Professors analysed student requests, and, in case of acceptance, they continued with a penalty of 15% in the final MT grade (i.e., MT2 equal to 85%). So, the MT final grade formula was avg(MT1, MT3)*85%.

2.4 Tools

All the tools explored ran online using the software as a service platform. The users (e.g., students) only need a computer, a tablet, or a smartphone to access the entire environment.

Teaching

ioEduc was initially developed in 2016 by TechTeach mentor. Its web-based features make it an excellent tool to support online classes (e-Learning).

In this CUnit, all the slides were available on this platform; students could, for example, ask questions, answer the quizzes, consult FAQs, access the drive, see their grades, or perform a peer assessment. Classes' attendances were also registered here through the attendances system. Drive had recorded classes and many books, tutorials, and videos to support the OT work. ioEduc also connects many complementary tools useful to help the working (e.g., Cloud 9 AWS, GitHub or Heroku). Professors uploaded all the content and applied gamification tasks here.

Table 1 shows the main features of ioEduc, and each user can do/access the platform. For example, a student can mark their presence. On the other hand, the teacher can see student attendance and assign bonuses.

Table 1 – ioEduc main features and users access adapted from (Silva, et al., 2020)

Feature	Teacher	Student
Mark presence in the class		X
See presences and assign bonus	X	
See class slides and other resource files	X	X
Manage slides and other resource files	X	
See software credentials	X	X
Manage software credentials	X	

Feature	Teacher	Student
See FAQ's	X	X
Manage FAQ's and FAQ's categories	X	
Create evaluation moments	X	
Submit student's grades for each evaluation moment	X	
See student's grades at each moment	X	
See only the logged user grades		X
Create and see quizzes on the ioQuiz tool and the results	X	
Submit and see the logged user ioQuiz grades		X
Create Kahoot quizzes and see the results	X	
Submit Kahoot quizzes		X
Create projects and teams	X	
Create groups	X	X
Evaluate group and each group member		X
See the logged user's group evaluations	X	X
See all the group evaluations	X	
Assign penalisation to students	X	
Create calendar events to a subject	X	
See calendar events of a subject		X
Manage Live Class	X	
Interact with live class	X	X
Ask questions on the integrated chat		X
Access and communicate through ioChat		

ioChat is based on open-source software. It is fully customised and has many features like messages/conversations (text, audio, and video), rooms (grouped, private, public or discussion), teams, notifications (online, email, push), plugins (drive, calendar, polls), among others.

ioChat was the primary communication tool and was integrated inside of ioEduc. The professor created several conversation rooms according to classes, teams, and groups.

At the beginning of each class (TP and LP), the professor started a video call to discuss the class goals with all the students. Then, all the students went to their respective room (Team or Group), initiated another video call, and started the work, which the professor accompanied (jumping between the rooms).

Zoom is a video-conferencing platform and supports the theoretical class. The professor started the recording and shared Zoom's ioEduc live system (containing the slides and other features). After a brief explanation of the week's main topics, the professor created several breakout rooms, and the students were randomly distributed. Students were faced with solving some challenges in a group according to the topics addressed in this phase. Before classes ending, all the students returned to the main room, and the professor performed a raffle among the attendees to determine which students had a bonus in the weekly quiz.

Assessment

We used two online interactive tools to perform the individual assessment synchronous tasks (MT1-MT3).

Kahoot! is a response system that engages participants through game-like pre-made or impromptu quizzes, discussions, and surveys and it was used in MT1&MT3. Students also used Kahoot and google forms (a final survey was available here) to perform professor and CUnit evaluation tasks.

HackerRank is a classic competitive programming platform with several different types of exercises and, it was used on MT2.

Developing Tools

To promote continuous and online learning, a set of well-known tools were available to students. They used GitHub to store and manage their code, AWSC9 or Visual Studio Code for programming, GitHub Pages and Heroku to support online project running and MySQL database.

Tools use

Figure 6 shows the main activities of each tool explored and the developing tools used.

2.5 Project

Project-Based learning is one of the best ways to achieve skills and learn through practice. The project developed tried to bring some innovation and entrepreneurship to the entire process and asked students to propose a possible solution to a real problem. The context of the project is explained in Figure 7.

Zoom
•Theoretical classes
•Share ioEduc live presentation system
•Breakout rooms with random groups
•Online recording
ioEduc
•Live presentation system (attendances, videos, clock, raffle, Kahoot, bonus, others)
•Responsive slides
•Registration of Teams, Groups, roles and leaders
•Registration of Attendances (presences)
•Individual grades by method
•Live Chat (ioChat)
•Drive and FAQs
•Survey (Live Kahoot) and Quiz
•Gamification tasks
•Connection with developing tools (integration or shortcut)
ioChat
•Direct messages
•Mail system
•TP and LP online classes
•Chat groups and rooms
•Teachers
•Group
•Team (All, FE, BE, FS)
•All
•Shifts
•Rules
•Technical Problems
Kahoot and Hacker Rank
•Individual assessment exercises
•Mini-Tests
•Evaluation (professor, CUnit assessment methods)
•Classes Survey
•Collect feedback from students
Developing Tools
•AWS C9
•GitHub
•GitHub Pages
•Heroku
•MySQL Workbench
•Visual Studio Code

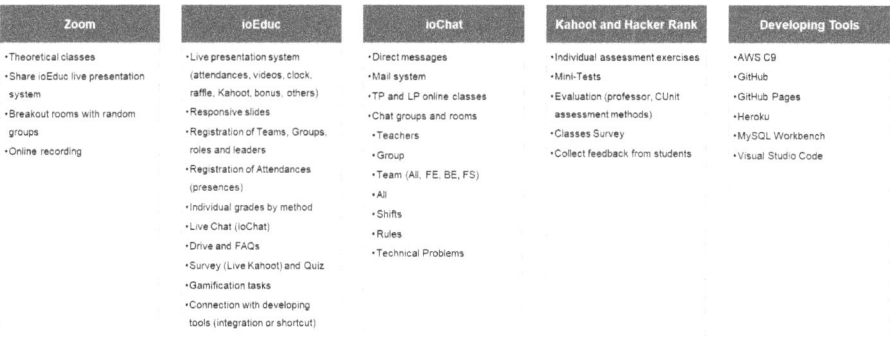

Figure 6 – Features and Tools

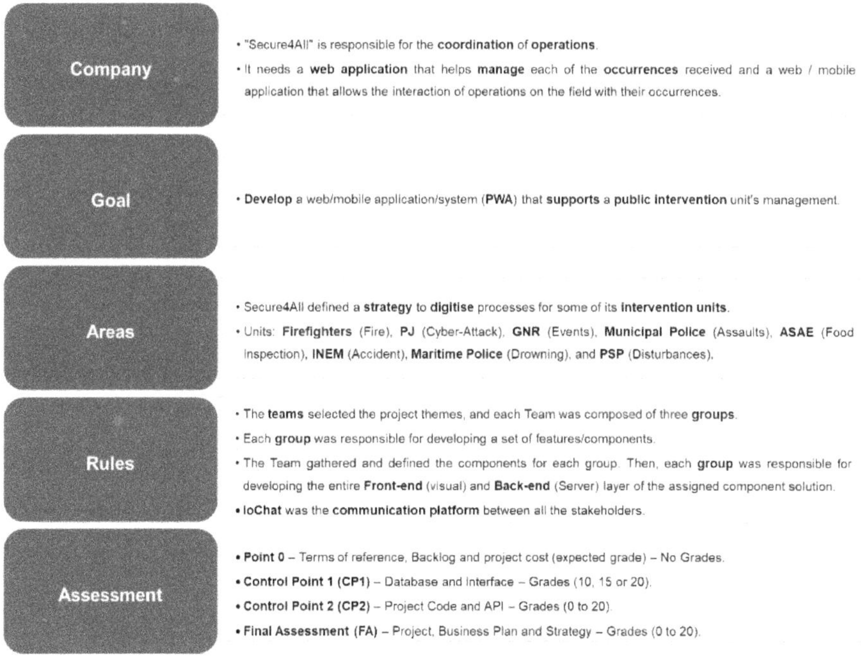

Company
• "Secure4All" is responsible for the coordination of operations.
• It needs a web application that helps manage each of the occurrences received and a web / mobile application that allows the interaction of operations on the field with their occurrences.
Goal
• Develop a web/mobile application/system (PWA) that supports a public intervention unit's management.
Areas
• Secure4All defined a strategy to digitise processes for some of its intervention units.
• Units: Firefighters (Fire), PJ (Cyber-Attack), GNR (Events), Municipal Police (Assaults), ASAE (Food Inspection), INEM (Accident), Maritime Police (Drowning), and PSP (Disturbances).
Rules
• The teams selected the project themes, and each Team was composed of three groups.
• Each group was responsible for developing a set of features/components.
• The Team gathered and defined the components for each group. Then, each group was responsible for developing the entire Front-end (visual) and Back-end (Server) layer of the assigned component solution.
• IoChat was the communication platform between all the stakeholders.
Assessment
• Point 0 – Terms of reference, Backlog and project cost (expected grade) – No Grades.
• Control Point 1 (CP1) – Database and Interface – Grades (10, 15 or 20).
• Control Point 2 (CP2) – Project Code and API – Grades (0 to 20).
• Final Assessment (FA) – Project, Business Plan and Strategy – Grades (0 to 20).

Figure 7 - Project statement

The main idea behind the project was to put students analysing a Portuguese Intervention Unit, study and comprehend their tasks and propose a solution to a particular operation. For example, some students contacted the Units and talked about their problems and desires. Then they filled terms of reference (workbook/specifications) with the professors by telling what they will do during the project and the cost (expected final project grade). After professors approved it, they started the work and developed an artefact to solve the problem identified. Professors evaluated the project according to the specifications and cost delivered by the students. This flow is similar to that a typical IT company have to follow when some customer asks for help/project. So, we confront the students with this reality inside the CUnit, anticipating their contact with the real world.

3. The challenges

The main challenge of the teaching is motivating the students to the classes and create an engaging environment. Several issues can arise during the online learning environment, so a list of possible risks (Figure 8) was defined, and the attenuating tasks were defined/implemented at the beginning.

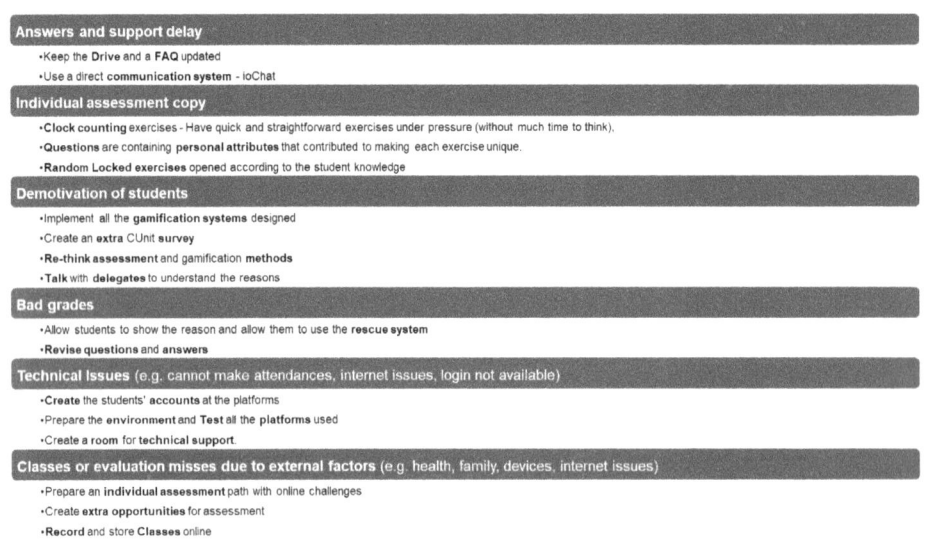

Figure 8 – Issues and solutions

4. How the initiative was received

The assessment moments were monitored, and three surveys were presented to the students asking their opinions about this initiative. We invited all the students to participate in the definition of the subject methods (Q1) and evaluate the CUnit (Q2&Q3). They were asked to participate in interactive surveys (Kahoot!) by answering questions about professors' performances, type of classes, motivation, expectations, among others. Questions like the type of classes or tests they prefer were also put to students during the classes. The evaluation followed the plan presented in Figure 9.

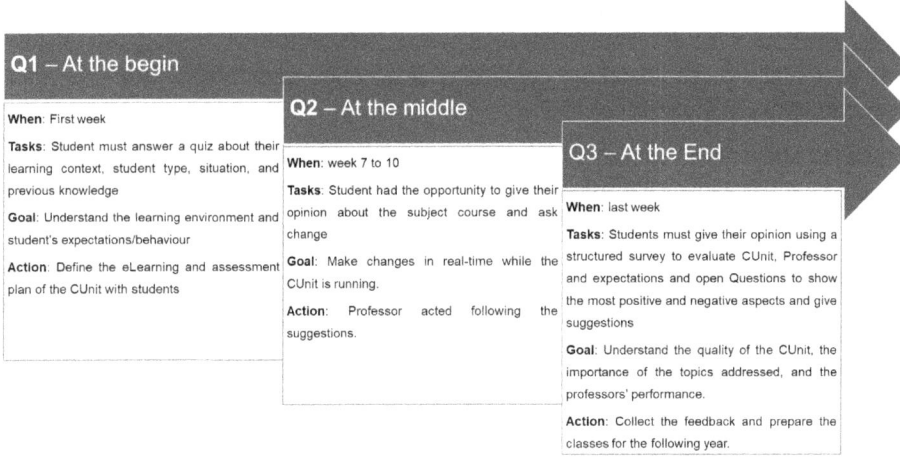

Figure 9 - CUnit Assessment phases

The student's answers and opinions are always used to make this CUnit more attractive and increase the student's engagement.

Regarding the CUnit, students' opinion was very positive and motivating. Figure 10 shows that more than ninety-five per cent of students (96,53%) considered this CUnit on the average or higher than average compared with other online subjects.

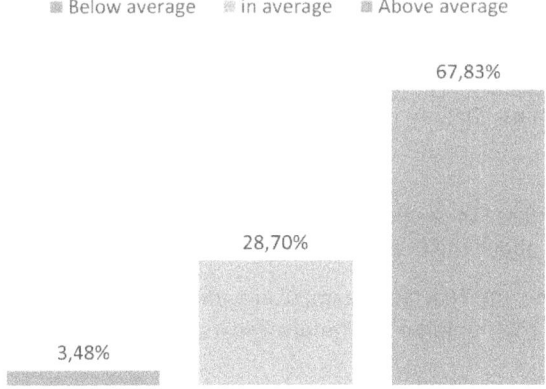

Figure 10 – How was this CUnit? (Portela, 2021)

In terms of the online class question (Figure 11), it is essential to mention that, although most of the students (60%) liked it, 40% answered "no". The negative answer was essentially due to working conditions (e.g., one computer at home to many users/students or lousy internet).

Figure 12 shows that 85% of students considered the gamification system Good or Excellent. In this aspect, it is essential to reveal student's opinions about MT. They liked MT1 and MT3 (62.39 % approved the model) but disliked MT2.

Both results showed the success of the strategy. MT1 and MT3 were easy and allowed professors to assess the basics knowledge. MT2 was challenging to copy or think, so the students did not like it. This situation led to having 15% of adverse opinions in the Gamification approach evaluation.

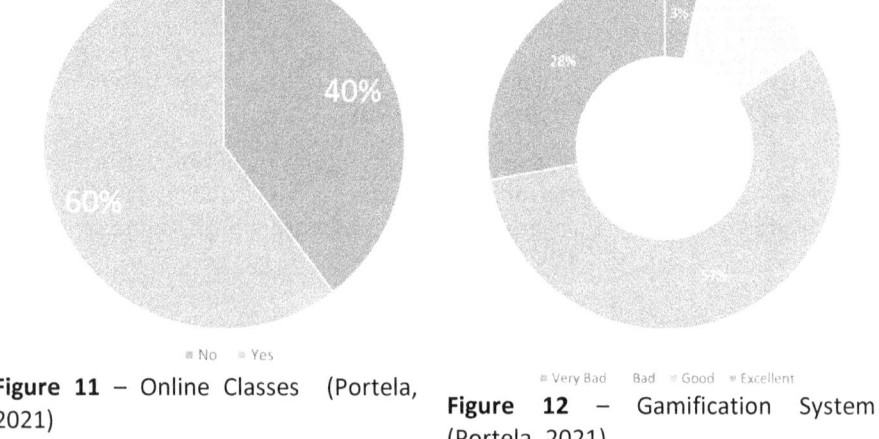

Figure 11 – Online Classes (Portela, 2021)

Figure 12 – Gamification System (Portela, 2021)

Figure 13 and Figure 14 shows the most positive and negative words regarding students' opinion about the CUnit.

On the positive side, the Teaching Team, CUnit, and TechTeach as one whole emerged. Students focused their opinion on the professors' availability and dynamism and the type of classes.

On the negative side, many answers were "nothing" to appoint. However, some students indicate some negative aspects of the quantity of matter and materials taught in the Theoretical classes - it happens because this CUnit is, unfortunately, the only one that addresses this thematic in the entire course.

Figure 13 – Positive aspects (Portela, 2021)

Figure 14 – Negative aspects (Portela, 2021)

Finally, Figure 15 shows students answers collected to the University Quality Report of the University of Minho. This report had 135 answers, and all the aspects analysed achieved more than 90% of positive answers.

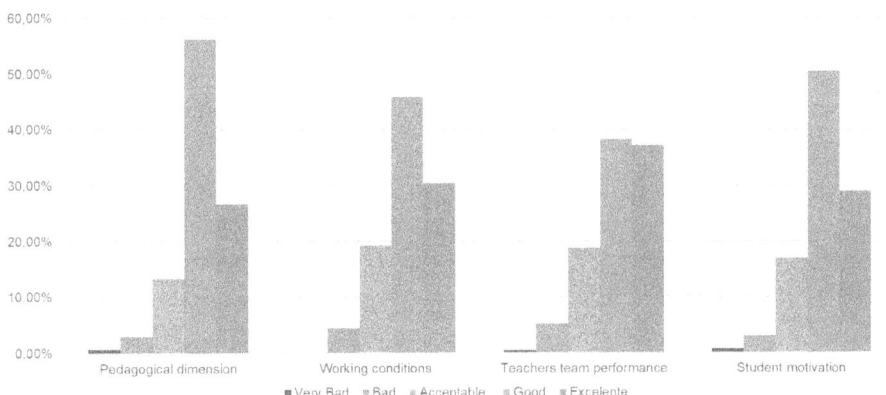

Figure 15 – CUnit Quality Report

Finally, two more questions were performed. First - Figure 16 - wanted to understand if ioEduc is valuable and should continue to be used to support the learning process. Then - Figure 17 – tried to understand if the students approved the concept of BYOD in the classroom, i.e., if the CUnit benefits from the use of personal devices (e.g. laptop or smartphone). In both cases, more than 85% of the students gave a positive answer.

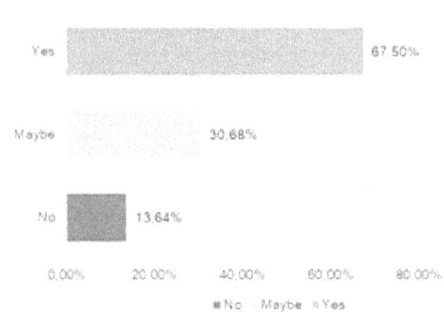

Figure 16. Should ioEduc be a gamble?   **Figure 17.** Do you approve BYOD concept?

5. The learning outcomes

The best way to show the impact of this initiative is by analysing the numbers and outcomes achieved with student's participation. We defined the learning outcomes by combining the teaching metrics (e.g., classes numbers, assessment methods and students results, student participation) with online traffic measures (e.g., sessions, page views, interactions). So, this initiative's learning outcomes were measured using digital metrics implemented inside ioEduc and ioChat combined with Google Analytics and semi-structured surveys (Q1-Q3).

Figure 18 and respective numbers help understand the impact and the effort needed to have a CUnit with a complete online learning environment. This figure splits measuring outcomes of e-Learning strategy into two big groups: Curricular Unit (CUnit) and Online Environment (e-Learning).

In the first group, it is possible to observe the number of shifts, assessment strategies, and the gamification approach. The second group shows the online numbers achieved from the environment created, the tools used, and the interactions observed.

Figures 19 to Figure 25 resume some of the numbers that were possible to achieve from ioEduc and ioChat (such as users by time or place, page views, events, sessions, among others) and presented in Figure 18. For example, the number of online users by some period (Figure 19) can show the students' participation in the classroom, the shifts with more students online, and their online engagement. Figure 19 shows an interesting and curious fact that only two periods (grey) did not have at least one student online during the entire CUnit.

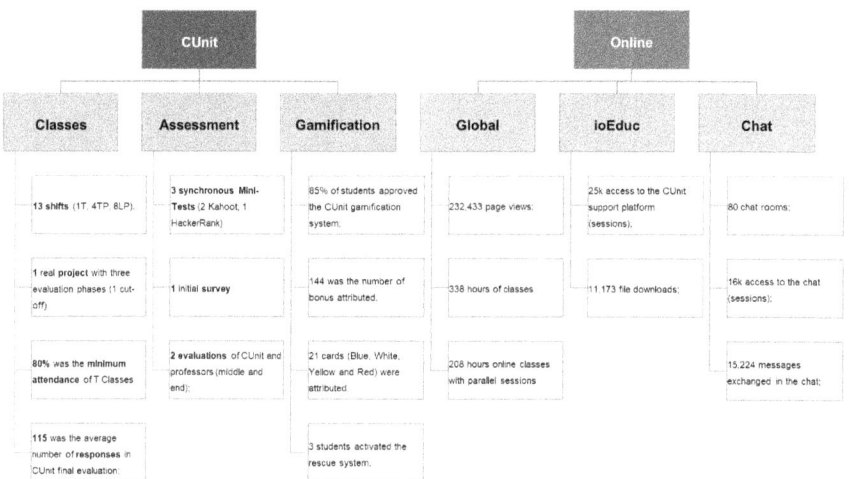

Figure 18 – TechTeach outcomes adapted from (Portela, 2021)

Figure 19 – Users by the time of day (Portela, 2021)

Figure 20 – Access by place

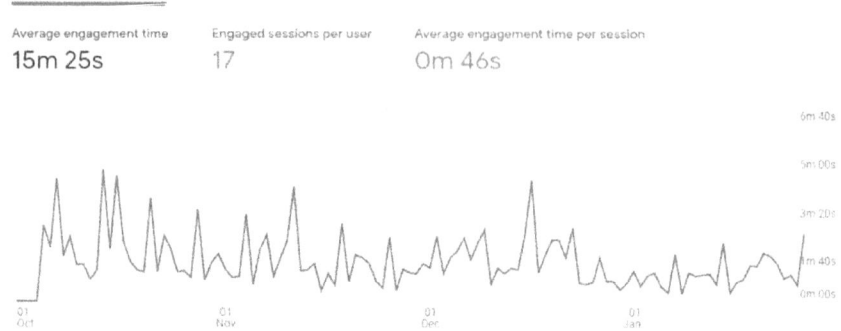

Figure 21 – Engaging time (Portela, 2021)

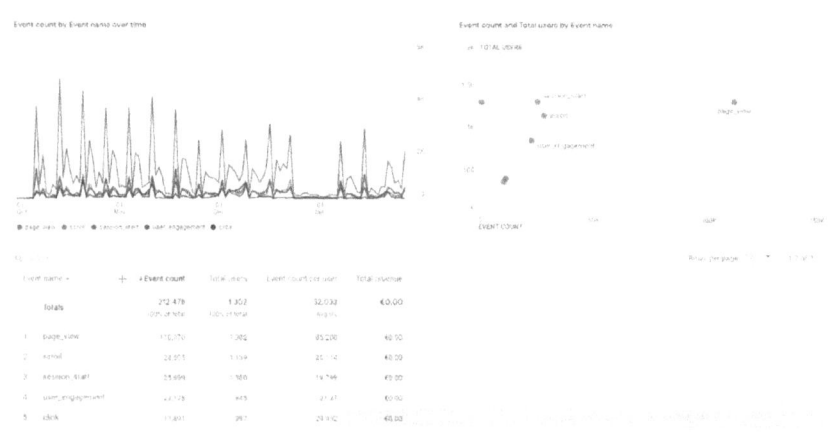

Figure 22 – ioEduc Online Events (Portela, 2021)

Figure 23 – ioChat events (Portela, 2021)

Figure 24 – ioChat most accessed channels

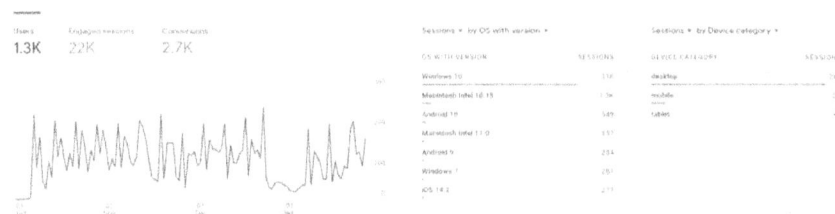

Figure 25 – ioChat user engagement

We can observe that the engaging level was impressive (22k engaged sessions). Students were not obligated to use the systems, participate in the classes, or even ask for help; however, most of them did that with pleasure and intending to learn more. The answer to RQ1 is yes. The use of TechTeach in an Online Environment can be considered a success (>80% positive answers).

Regarding Q2, it is vital to highlight the effort need to be put into practice. For example, the coordinator' effort was 250%*teachingHours(8) in an average of 20h/week. However, it was strong compensated by the excellent results achieved:

- more than 220k page views,
- 40k sessions,
- 11k downloads of files,
- 15k messages
- 95% of approved students.

Unfortunately, this study also showed a considerable gap. In some cases, and although the results are motivating, students affirmed not having good learning conditions at home and fear/distrust online classes.

TechTeach is adequate to the constantly changing teaching system; it brings fresh air to e-Learning, and it has a favourable acceptance (>95% positive answers). Finally, three articles were already published to disseminate this paradigm through the community:

- TechTeach - An innovative method to increase student engagement at classrooms (Portela, 2020).
- A new and interactive teaching approach with Gamification for motivating students in computer science classrooms (Portela, 2020)
- Online-teaching environment with Gamification - A real case study (Portela, 2021).

6. Conclusion

TechTeach was designed for several years and showed promising results in a presential and non-presential contact environment. In order to assess the online approach and verify if the main goals were met, some results must be highlighted:

- Both stakeholders (students and professors) considered this approach a success (>80% positive answers).
- More than 95% of students considered this CUnit equal or better than the other online subjects.
- 20h/week was the effort needed to put this approach into practice.
- Gamification reveals to be a promising approach to motivate students to keep them active, receive feedback and improve their grades (>85% positive answers).
- 95% of the active students (i.e., attended at least 1/3 of the entire planned classes) got approved with an average grade of 15.83.

In a final analysis, the two goals were fully met, and the achieved results are much rewarding and offset the effort. So, we can conclude that TechTeach is a disruptive approach that works well in an e-learning environment and primarily focuses on the students' performance and motivation. Although this paradigm is toolless, ioEduc combined with ioChat was revealed to be a fantastic e-learning tool and achieved the students' final approval. This case study showed that it is possible to have online classes and keep the students engaged. The key to success is in the learning ecosystem created, i.e., in the mode of how the professors dynamise the environment, allowing the use of technologies and innovative approaches like Gamification or professional challenges/experiences to potentiate learning and support the teaching.

Research communities and professors should see this contribution as a guideline with good practices for innovating and proportionating interactive online learning environments. I hope this case study can help other professors in the digital transition process and motivate them to promote a new type of learning that is fully interactive and use Gamification to engage students in the classrooms and turn them into better professionals.

7. Plans to further develop the initiative

In the future, collected data will be dissected, and Web Mining techniques will be applied to correlate the students' performance with their online activity. Concerning TechTeach, the goal is to continue their improvement, explore it in different contexts and optimise ioEduc - to turn it more global, available to other teams/professors and add more gamification methods by following some of the suggestions received.

Then, a new approach will be explored soon. In a brief explanation, students will have to choose one learning path from the available two. The first path is for students who only want to learn the basics, do not want to have much effort, and do not want to achieve high grades. The second path is for students who wish to explore more, acquire expert knowledge, and obtain excellent rates. Both tracks will explore a flipped grade system. The idea is to revolutionise how the students are evaluated and create a narrative to include all the assessment tasks.

Acknowledgements

A special thanks to the School of Engineering at the University of Minho, which motivated and allowed us to innovate the teaching process and IOTECH to help the development of Gamification tools. This work has been supported by FCT – Fundação para a Ciência e Tecnologia within the R&D Units Project Scope: UIDB/00319/2020

References

Portela, F., 2020. TechTeach - An innovative method to increase the student's engagement at classrooms. Information - Special Issue "Computer Programming Education". Volume 11, 2020, Issue 10 . ISSN: 2078-2489.

Portela, F., 2020. A new and interactive teaching approach with Gamification for motivating students in computer science classrooms. Vila do Conde, OASIcs.

Portela, F., 2021. Online-teaching environment with Gamification - A real case study. University of Minho, OpenAccess Series in Informatics, 91, art. no. 1. 978-3-95977-194-8. OASIcs.

Silva, M., Ferreira, D. & Portela, F., 2020. ioEduc-Bring your own device to the classroom. Vila do Conde, OASIcs.

Author biography

Filipe Portela is an Invited Assistant Professor at the University of Minho, an Integrated Researcher of Algoritmi Centre and the founder and CEO of IOTECH- Innovation on Technology. He researches/works/teaches in areas like Gamification, Web Programming and Data Science and is the author/editor of many articles/journals/books in these area

Enhancing Student's Practical Skills with Modified Flipped Classroom (MFC) Approach using UFUTURE

Prasanna Ramakrisnan
Institute of Continuing Education & Professional Studies and Faculty of Computer and Mathematical Sciences, Universiti Teknologi MARA, Shah Alam, Selangor, Malaysia

prasanna@uitm.edu.my

Abstract: When the universities across the globe were instructed to be closed due to the COVID-19 outbreak, teaching and learning could not also be stopped abruptly. Educators therefore had to shift their teaching instructions into a fully online environment within relatively short notice in response to the pandemic. However, there was lack of guidance on how to move the existing huge number of courses to online and how best to deliver the content effectively to close to 170,000 students during pandemic. This e-learning initiative presents a custom designed learning management system named UFUTURE that supports instructors to design their course instructions for blended learning (BL), open and distance learning (ODL), MOOCS and Microcredential during and post pandemic at Universiti Teknologi MARA (UiTM). The instructors were encouraged to use UFUTURE in fully online course delivery during pandemic. In the MFC approach, the classroom time is converted to synchronous online class and asynchronous problem-solving activities. The MFC approach comprises asynchronous online learning activities (self-paced learning activities, pre-recorded video content, lecture notes, and online discussion boards) and synchronous online learning activities (online class and discussions). UFUTURE supported and monitored student participations in both synchronous and asynchronous online learning activities. The MFC proposes five steps to design the course learning instructions. While developing the course instructions and materials, 5 components of the self-developed model (DeLCAD: Teaching Delivery, Learning Activities, Course Content, Assessment and Discussion) were used as a guide. The identified major challenge in implementing this approach was internet connectivity for the students. The effectiveness of the modified flipped classroom approach using UFUTURE was based on two indicators (i) student's feedback and (ii) student's practical skills performance. Courses that design using the MFC approach provide greater flexibility in student learning and improves their achievement.

1. Introduction

There are currently five (5) modes for teaching delivery including traditional face-to-face, web-facilitated, blended, fully online, and emergency remote. The traditional face-to-face mode is when an instructor teaches a group of students in person. Web-enhanced courses are traditional courses that have some technology-mediated components that complement the required class meetings, for example, online quiz or discussions [1, 2]. Blended courses are between 30% to 80% of course instructions delivered online with some face-to-face instructions [3]. A widely known type of blended learning is the 'flipped classroom'. The flipped classroom is a pedagogical model that reverses the typical lecture and homework elements of a course. The students are introduced to the content asynchronously before the class session. Then class time is used for active learning such as discussions, problem-solving, or lab-based activities [e.g., 4].

Courses where more than 80% of the course content is delivered online are referred to as fully online courses. Fully online courses are conducted solely online using virtual instructions with the components of face-to-face instructions are provided online. Emergency remote courses are courses that instructors temporarily shift the instructional delivery to an alternate delivery mode due to crisis circumstances. Blended, online and emergency remote courses are redefining the traditional instructor role in the teaching organization and delivery process [e.g., 5].

1.1 Pre-Planning

There are a few things to consider before moving the existing traditionally taught courses in higher education online. Among them are: (1) examine student readiness for remote learning and choose the most relevant tools based on student accessibility, and (2) modify course plan for remote learning.

1. Examine student readiness for remote learning and choose the most relevant tools based on student accessibility

The readiness of students and their accessibility for online learning can be measured through a survey. The survey questions were based on five sections including (1) internet accessibility, (2) learning technology accessibility, (3) online learning preference, (4) online learning experience, and (5) readiness. This survey is conducted to assist decision-making on the high-technology or low-technology solutions based on internet connectivity and digital skills of the students.

2. Modify course plan for remote learning

The course plan is then modified so that course learning outcomes can achieved timely during emergencies such as the COVID-19 pandemic. The learning outcomes developed for a traditional face-to-face can still be met if the course is moved online.

1.2 Designing Teaching Instructions

MFC instructions are a combination of asynchronous and synchronous teaching delivery. For example, the Computer and Information Processing course (code: CSC134) is offered to part-time students at UiTM. This course is conducted using the ODL MFC approach through an interactive online platform coupled with limited synchronous online classes.

However, the student learning time (SLT) for CSC134 part-time is still the same as full-time. It is a 3-hour credit course with 4-hour contact per week for 14 weeks. In traditional face-to-face mode, 28 hours is allocated for face-to-face lectures and 28 hours for face-to-face lab sessions, making a total of 56 hours or 100% of the face-to-face delivery. On the other hand, the delivery mode for CSC134 is a combination of synchronous online classes and asynchronous online learning activates using ODL modified flipped classroom approach. About 10 hours (18%) of synchronous online classes and 46 hours of asynchronous online learning activates are allocated, making 100% of the teaching delivery is in the online mode.

The 5 steps for designing modified flipped classroom instructions are: (1) Identify the instructional components, (2) Plan course structure and instructional strategies, (3) Develop the course instructions and material, (4) Implement the instructional course materials, (5) Assess the effectiveness of the course instructions.

Step 1: Identify the instructional component

The instructional components for ODL modified flipped classroom approach are based on the synchronous online class and asynchronous online learning activities. The contact hours for synchronous online classes (online classroom instructions) are 10 hours (5 seminars). And the remaining hours (46 hours) will be for asynchronous online learning activities (online learning instructions).

The online classroom instructions are designed for each seminar based on 2 hours contact. The online classroom instructional components were planned as below for every seminar with 2 contact hours.

- Online classroom learning activities (45 minutes)
- Online reflection activity (15 minutes)
- Online individual or group exercises (60 minutes)

While the online learning instructional components were planned as below for the remaining 46 contact hours.

- Online self-paced asynchronous learning activities (4 hours x 9 topics = 36 hours)
- Online self-paced learning for technology tools (2 hours x 5 tools = 10 hours)

Step 2: Plan course structure and instructional strategies

The course structure needs to be outlined based on the identified instructional strategies, i.e. synchronous online class (10 hours) and asynchronous online learning activities (46 hours).

Some changes are required in student-instructor, student-content, and student-student interactions for online classroom transitioning.

1. *Student-instructor interaction:* the changes in learning schedule, assignment due dates and assessment dates communicated clearly to the students. The method used to communicate with the students was the What's App group message. Separate individual messages also send to those students who are not active in their online learning to understand their constraints. Below are some of the interactions done with the students:
   - Communicate with students using the same method that is What's App.
   - Students will be notified in the system and WhatsApp message when a new assessment is added.
   - The i-Discuss (discussion board) feature in UFUTURE is utilized to respond to students' doubts on the topic of learning. Students will be always encouraged to check the i-Discuss before What's App for any doubts.
   -
   - *Student-content interaction:* Additional course materials were shared as students have to self-learn remotely. Below instructions were given to students when new course material was posted.
   - Students were notified of the availability of course materials.
   - Suggest students to identify and share additional learning material that meets their learning outcomes.
   - Course materials were converted to PDF format to allow the students to access those materials using mobile devices.
   - Copy of course materials always shared in class What's App group for easy content accessibility.
2. *Student-student interaction:* Communication between the students is fostered using i-Discuss in UFUTURE and other learning technology tools. Below are some of the activities used to foster student-to-student interactions.
   - Students always engaged in live discussion during the online synchronous session.
   - Students also always engaged in discussion among other students in i-Discuss during the online asynchronous session.

- A set of online collaboration tools (Google and Jam board) was introduced to facilitate students' online group assignments and collaboration tasks.

Step 3: Develop the course instructions and material

In developing the course instructions and materials for CSC134, 5 components of the self-developed model (DeLCAD: Teaching Delivery (De), Learning Activities (L), Course Content (C), Assessment (A) and Discussion (D)) were used as a guide [6]. The online classroom instructions were developed for the synchronous online class and online learning instructions were developed for asynchronous online learning activities.

Online class instructions: The online class instructions for the seminar are explained by DeLCAD. Using the online teaching delivery method, learning activities will be designed in a facilitated and fun mode so that the students will be motivated to participate. Take note that designing online class instructions are limited to time. Thus, a combination of some activities from learning activities / course content / assessment / discussion can be used to design the online class instructions. Figure 1 shows an example of teaching planning for a seminar using online seminar delivery strategies.

SEMINAR 1
LO:
At the end of the seminar:
1. student will be able to understand the concepts and components of computer (CLO1)
2. student will be able to use the most popular and current application software (CLO6)

Teaching Delivery for Seminar 1 : Online Face-to-Face
Total contact hours : 2 hours (120 minutes)

Learner's Task	Delivery Strategy	L	C	A	D	Delivery Tool(s)
INTERACTIVITY FOCUSED Students participate in the *Classroom Learning Activity 01* (refer below) (45 minutes)	Collaborative information sharing	/				Zoom (Breakout Room) Jamboard
REFLECTION FOCUSED Student are assessed with *Exercise 01* on their understanding related to Classroom Learning Activity 01 (15 minutes)	Educational games			/		Zoom Kahoot!
ONLINE LECTURE FOCUSED Students taught to use application software to solve the problem in *Lab Exercise 1* (60 minutes)	Problem solving exercise			/		Zoom Canva Adobe Spark

L= Learning Activity, C= Course Content, A= Assessment, D= Discussion

Figure 1. Teaching plan for seminar 1 using DeLCAD model

Online learning instructions: The teaching instructions for student's online learning are also explained by using DeLCAD. Using the online teaching delivery method, learning activities will be designed in facilitated and self-paced engaging mode so that the students will participate online. Parts of the lessons also can be delivered online using pre-recorded video. Online assessment tools like quizzes, tests and assignment rubrics can be used to assess student's understanding and quality of their project. Students also use the online discussion tools to discuss project development matters asynchronously between other students and the lecturer. Figure 2 shows sample for one week of detailed teaching planning for self-paced online learning.

TOPIC 1 INTRODUCTION

TLO:
1. Define the term, computer, and describe the relationship between data and information
2. Describe the different types of computer hardware, including the system unit, input, output, storage, and communication devices.
3. Identify the four types of computers and the four types of personal computers.
4. Explain the parts of an information system: people, procedures, software, hardware, data, and the Internet.
5. Discuss how society uses computers in education, finance, government, health care, science, publishing, travel, and manufacturing

Teaching Delivery for Topic 1 : Self-Paced Online Learning
Total contact hours : 4 hours (240 minutes)

Week	Topic(s)	Learner's Task	Delivery Strategy	L	C	A	D	Delivery Tool(s)
Week 1 At the end of the week, student will be able to understand the concepts and components of computer (CLO1)	• Introduction to Computer (TLO1) • Component of a computer (TLO2) • Types of computers (TLO3) • Computer in society (TLO5) • Information systems (TLO4) • Your future, careers and opportunities (TLO5)	CONTENT FOCUSED Student self-learn *e-content* for Topic 1 and update their self-learning in Trello board (120 minutes)	Student-led learning	/				UFUTURE Trello
		INTERACTIVITY FOCUSED Students participate in the *online learning activities* designed by the instructor (30 minutes)	Educational Games	/					UFUTURE TOGlic H5P
		INTERACTIVITY FOCUSED Students participate in Topic 1 *asynchronous online discussion* questions posted by instructor (60 minutes)	Discussion Panel				/	UFUTURE
		REFLECTION FOCUSED Student self-assess their understanding on Topic 1 by answering *online self-assessment.* (30 minutes)	Self-Assessment			/		UFUTURE Quizzes

**e-content (10 min lecture video / 12 slides) = 1-hour traditional face-to-face lecture*
**L= Learning Activity, C= Course Content, A= Assessment, D= Discussion*

Figure 2. Teaching plan for weekly self-paced online learning using DeLCAD model

Step 4: Implement the instructional course material

The instructional course materials for CSC134 were developed using digital education tools like h5p, quizzes and etc. Then, all the developed instructional course materials and activities are delivered to students using platforms such as the UFUTURE.

Step 5: Assess the effectiveness of the course instruction.

There is a range of models that can be used to obtain reflection on student learning experience in their course instructions. The course instructions were assessed using an online feedback form and student performance in the skill-based task given.

Besides that, the student's actual participation in both synchronous and asynchronous learning activities were monitored using costume design monitoring tool in UFUTURE. The online class can be conducted inside UFUTURE or any platform like Zoom, Google Meet, Webex and etc. The online class attendance taking and analytic reporting can be generated in UFUTURE. While for the asynchronous online learning activities, detail reporting in student participation in learning activities and discussion can be also generated inside UFUTURE.

The effectiveness of the course instruction delivery using MFC approach can be measured through student performance in achieving the course learning outcomes. To assist the instructors in identifying student performance in their learning, a set of customize reporting such as rubric analytic reporting, progress and performance reporting, student assessment gradebook and assessment progress monitoring in UFUTURE are used.

2. The Infrastructure

The modified flipped approach replaces instructor lectures with online instructional materials. The student will interact and learn using those materials outside classroom sessions. The **people** that are involved in this implementation are the instructors and their students.

There are many **digital tools** used for flipped lessons outside the classroom and engagement during online class time. Some of the tools used for creating instructional materials are PowerPoint, iMovie, LOOM, PowToon, Canva, and Adobe Spark. While to create student learning activities, tools like H5P, Jamboard, Kahoot!, Quizizz, Mentimeter, Zoom Breakout Rooms, TOGlic, Padlet, and Trello were used. Both the instructional materials and learning activities were embedded into UiTM learning management system (UFUTURE).

A few additional **hardware** required to record the instructional videos. Basic hardware like webcam, microphone, portable lighting was used for recording. Thus, not much **cost** is involved in implementing the MFC approach for any course delivery.

3. The Challenges in implementing MFC Approach

Below are some of the challenges and solutions used when implementing the MFC approach.

3.1 Lack of internet connectivity

The biggest challenge during remote teaching was student internet connectivity. Some of the students were unable to join online synchronous classes.

Solution: Upload the activities in Padlet, UFUTURE, and WhatsApp so that students can retrieve those activities based on their accessibility.

3.2 Structure of traditional lab session difficult to be flipped

Fostering practical skills among students in remote teaching can be quite difficult. It's impossible to see if the students have attained the required skills.

Solution: Provide with entrance and exit survey for every online class session that involves the attainment of certain skills. By this, the instructor was able to identify those areas that need intervention. Extra material and exercises were given to achieve those required skills.

3.3 Lack of resources

Some students having difficulty using their laptops or PC complete their practical tasks. Their devices are either too old or not available at all.

Solution: Proposed customized virtualize desktop (VD) for students with lack of computing resources. The proposed VD is integrated with the UFUTURE private cloud.

4. Student Feedback

Qualitative assessment based on student online feedback regarding the course delivery. This feedback is on student perception toward a course delivered using the MFC approach. Five questions were asked on this feedback to gather student's thoughts on how the MFC approach affected their learning.

Case Study 1:

74 students enrolled in 3 different courses participated in this feedback. All the 3 courses (Computer and Information Processing, Interactive Multimedia, and Fundamentals to Multimedia Computing) had a minimum of one learning outcome that requires practical skill attainment and delivered using the MFC approach. The 74 collected student responses were summarised in Figure 3.

Course delivery method

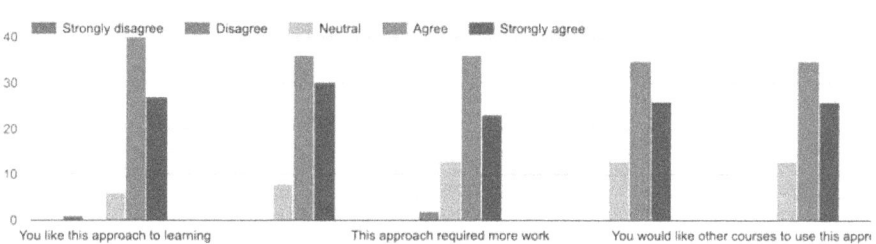

Figure 3. Students' responses toward course delivery using the MFC approach

Case Study 2:

42 students enrolled in the Fundamentals to Multimedia Computing course have participated in this study. The students were divided into 2 groups: 21 students in the experiment group (MFC approach) and another 21 students in the control group (teacher-centered approach). The same 5 questions were distributed in an online feedback form and the data was collected as shown in Table 1.

Table 2. Data collection from student online feedback form

Questions	Experiment Group Mean	Control Group Mean
You like this approach to learning.	4.45	3.85
This approach helped you to understand the topics better.	4.40	3.95
This approach required more work.	4.45	3.70
You would like more of the topics in the course taught this way.	4.35	3.80
You would like other courses to use this approach to learning.	4.20	3.75

The overall finding from both the case study indicated the students mostly said that they like the approach and that they also understand better although this approach requires more of their effort. They also indicated that they prefer this approach for remaining of the course topics and to be applied in other courses too.

5. Learning Outcome Attainment and Measure

Table 2 below are the details of courses that used the MFC approach, the targeted learning outcome (LO) related to practical skills, student's tasks used to measure the LO, and methods used to measure the LO.

Table 3. Course learning outcome, assessment method, and measurement

Course Name	Targeted LO	Assessment Method	Measurement
Computer and Information Processing	LO1: Follow the use of current business software for various application in the industry.	Group assignment to use presentation software	Presentation rubric
Interactive Multimedia	LO2: Demonstrate appropriate design and social interaction with team members and society through the development of multimedia project	Group assignment to design and develop an interactive multimedia project	Interactive multimedia development rubric
Fundamentals to Multimedia Computing	LO3: Constructs practical skills in fundamental of multimedia computing	Group assignment to create an animated short story	Pre-production materials rubric and animated short story rubric

The performance-based task in the form of assignments assigned to assess student practical skill learning. Performance-based assignments used rubrics to evaluate the series of criteria that were needed to complete the assigned task. A well-written rubric will provide a clear expectation of the assignment. Figure 4 shows the designed screen inside UFUTURE to construct the rubrics for the assignments.

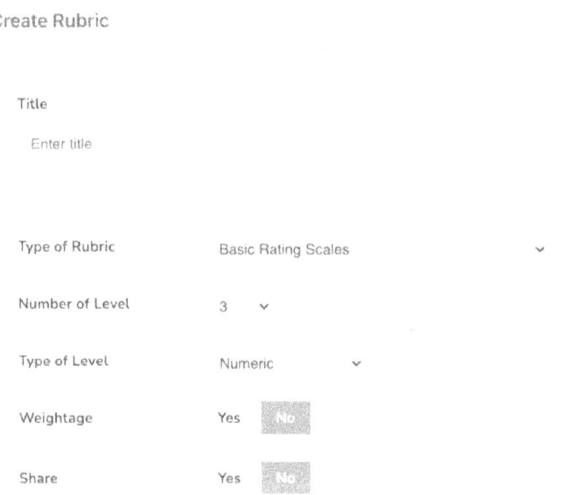

Figure 4. Screen to construct a rubric

The learning outcomes in Table 2 are measured using group assignments. The group assignment is assigned to the students in UFUTURE. The entire process of assigning, rubric-based marking, and student feedback for the assignment were design into UFUTURE based on my proposed process and screen design. The detailed analysis of the rubric for each of the assignments will reveal the overall performance of students in attaining the desired learning outcome. The analysis can be used to improve the teaching process for better achievement of the learning outcome.

Figure 5 shows the rubric analytic for assessment of LO1. The analysis provides the performance gap; the difference between the intended and actual performance of each criterion. The range of performance gap was 0%-25%. The criteria with bigger gaps were paid attention and extra materials were given to the student to close or minimize the gap. The LO2 and LO3 have also scored a lower performance gap (<30%). Thus, this teaching delivery using the MFC approach can be used to teach practical skill-based courses.

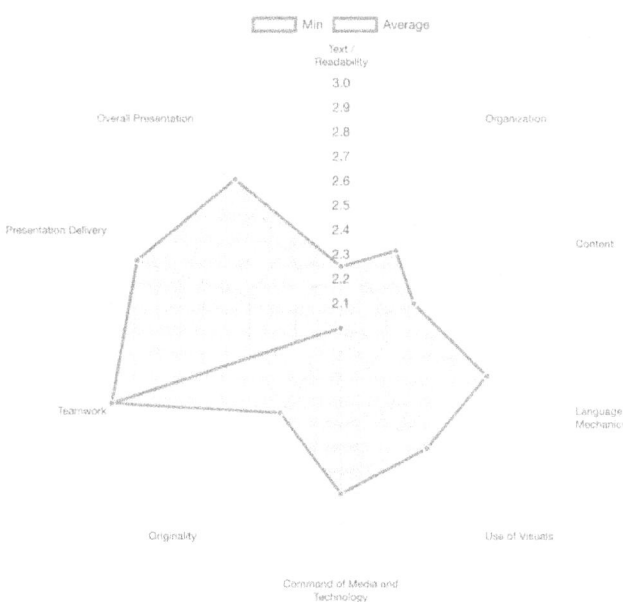

Criteria/Point	Min	Max	Average
Text / Readability	2.00	3.00	2.25
Organization	2.00	3.00	2.39
Content	2.00	3.00	2.52
Language Mechanics	2.00	3.00	2.64
Use of Visuals	2.00	3.00	2.61
Command of Media and Technology	2.00	3.00	2.68
Originality	2.00	3.00	2.41
Teamwork	3.00	3.00	3
Presentation Delivery	2.00	3.00	2.59
Overall Presentation	2.00	3.00	2.75

Average Student Mark : 25.86

Figure 5. Rubric analytic screen

6. Future Plans

This case discusses the 5 steps for designing a course in UFUTURE using the MFC approach. The summary of the 5 steps is given in Figure 6.

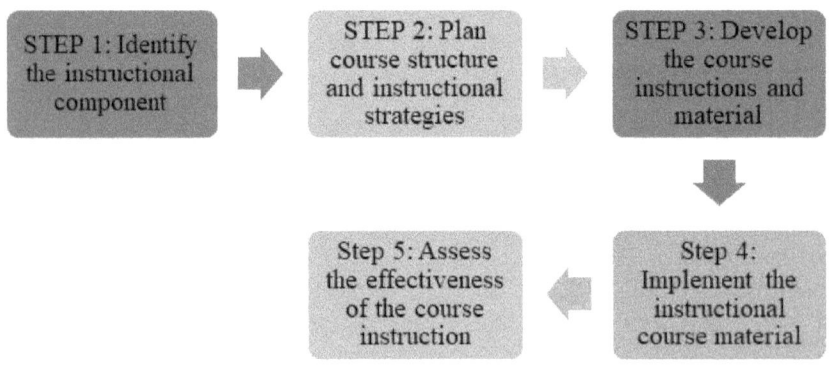

Figure 6. The 5 steps to design a course using modified flipped classroom (MFC) approach

These 5 steps also can be applied for designing teaching instructions for the traditional or blended learning-based courses. Courses that design using the MFC approach provide greater flexibility in student learning and improves their achievement. The developed UFUTURE platform supports the implementation of MFC approach in teaching and learning at UiTM . This approach also enhances the student learning experience by creating opportunities for students to improve their understanding through self-paced learning. The future plan is to provide more training and awareness to instructors on how to implement the MFC approach in course delivery using UFUTURE. Besides that, future study is also to look into the impact of the MFC approach on aspects of the student learning experience in a university course.

References

W. Kang and I, Kim, "A comparison of blended learning and traditional face-to-face learning for some dental technology students in practice teaching," J. Tech. Dent., vol. 42, pp. 248–253, 2020. https://doi.org/10.14347/jtd.2020.42.3.248

A. Ahlam, K. Aryn C., L. Andrew and B. Jacob, "Online and face-to-face classroom multitasking and academic performance: Moderated mediation with self-efficacy for self-regulated learning and gender," Comps. in Human Behavior, vol. 102, pp. 214–222, 2020. https://doi.org/10.1016/j.chb.2019.08.018.

B. Nayar, and S. Koul, "Blended learning in higher education: a transition to experiential classrooms", Intl. J. Edu. Mngmt., vol. 34, pp. 1357–1374, 2020. https://doi.org/10.1108/IJEM-08-2019-0295

E. Colomo-Magaña, R. Soto-Varela, J. Ruiz-Palmero and M. Gómez-García, "University students' perception of the usefulness of the flipped classroom methodology," Educ. Sci., vol. 10, pp. 275–294, 2020.

A. P. Aguilera-Hermida, "College students' use and acceptance of emergency online learning due to COVID-19," Intl. J. Edu. Res. Open, vol. 1, p. 100011, 2020.https://doi.org/10.1016/j.ijedro.2020.100011.

R. Prasanna, Nor Aziah Alias and N. V., "Designing Blended Learning for Skill-Based Course: Introducing DeLCAD Model for Course Design," in M.K.Y. Chan, S.E. Ling and S.C. Ling (Eds). Blended Learning in Teacher Training – Innovation and Good Practices, Proceedings of 1st International Conference on Education in the Ecosystem, pp. 379 – 385 (ISBN: 978-1-60595-658-9), August 19 – 22, 2019, Kuching, Sarawak, Malaysia.

Author biography

Prasanna Ramakrisnan is a Senior Lecturer at Faculty of Computer and Mathematical Sciences, UiTM and holds an academic administrative position as Head of Information Technology Division at the Institute of Continuing Education & Professional Studies (iCEPS). She played an important role in the development of UFUTURE.

Coventry University Virtual World Tour

Alex Regan and Albina Szeles
Centre for Global Engagement, Coventry University, UK
aa4040@coventry.ac.uk
ab1244@coventry.ac.uk

1. Introduction

Restrictions imposed by the global pandemic have negatively impacted internationalisation across the higher education sector, with students among those most affected as they have missed opportunities to travel, discover new cultures and develop professional networks. Coventry University has been 1st for Overseas Student Experiences for 6 years running, based on student trips abroad from HESA 2014/15-2019/20 UK with over 6000 students undertaking mobility abroad in a year prior to the pandemic. Despite challenges teams at the university showed their dedication to continue creating global graduates, by innovating and collaborating with overseas institutions on an immersive virtual mobility experience called the Virtual World Tour. The Virtual World Tour was designed with the following objectives:

- • to create a global community of learning
- •to develop students' global knowledge and competencies while increasing confidence and enthusiasm for future travel
- • to build and develop relationships with other universities and institutions

Over 1,500 participants joined the Virtual World Tour over a four-month period. A dedicated 'hub' allowed participants to book onto a variety of live sessions and workshops as well as access on demand activities, recordings and resources enabling virtual travel experience to 25 countries. The project offered access to live language and culture sessions, leadership seminars to develop transferable skills, and a variety of workshops delivered by both Coventry University staff and those from other institutions all over the world. In addition, LinkedIn Learning supported the project, helping to enhance student employability through cultural competencies. To create an inclusive and truly global project, access to the Virtual World Tour was offered to students and staff at more than 40 overseas Higher Education Institutions (HEIs) welcoming students from all continents and subject disciplines

2. Infrastructure

2.1 The team

A small team managed a range of aspects linked to the project from its inception to review, including design of the VWT hub and specific country tour content, marketing and social media campaigns, partnership development and management, webinar scheduling, technical support, certificate design and distribution, country/ cultural research and design and response to participant queries.

2.2 External institutions

Engagement with external institutions was key to creating the community of learning and the success of the project. The team at Coventry University had significant experience in Collaborative Online International Learning projects (COIL) as well as collaborations with Study abroad and Transnational Education partners, which helped to strengthen the collaboration during those unprecedented times.

The response we received was overwhelming. Over 40 external institutions agreeing to support with promoting the VWT to their students and delivering webinars as part of the project. The webinars were based around culture and sustainability, which are international learning objectives for students. A list of all participating external institutions including HEIs is featured in the acknowledgement section.

The contribution of local perspectives and cultural resources from HEI staff as well as from students through interactive activities has supported truly global classroom from comfort and safety of homes

2.3 Hub landing page

To support the digital innovation of the project a designated hub landing page was created to ensure student engagement. For this purpose, Open Moodle was deemed an appropriate choice, given both Coventry University and several external institutions were familiar with the learning environment.

Through Open Moodle, we were also able to create discussion forums which students engaged with, sharing their cultural insights. Interactive tiles were designed representing a different destination of the tour (25 in total). Each tile also provided an immersive virtual environment for students to explore; we added videos, quizzes, case studies, pictures, text and embedded links to virtual walking tours or virtual museums. These resources combined provided a wealth of materials for students to expand their cultural competencies.

2.4   Additional digital literacies

Although the hub provided an excellent reference point to start students on their Virtual World Tour, additional digital literacies were incorporated to support the range of activities including:

- **Webinar booking system:** allowing the team to manage the number of participants for each event, and manage a reminder system to increase engagement whilst ensuring GDPR compliancy

- **Microsoft Teams/Zoom:** allowing students to listen, watch and engage with speakers across the world

- **Plotagon (app):** for designing informative virtual flight videos presenting key information and facts about each destination and allowing each participant to feel that they were "taking flight"

- **Genial:** a virtual escape room was designed based on sustainability, the escape room allowed students to explore sustainability themes in a fun and innovative way

- **Kahoot/Padlet:** providing opportunities for students to evidence their cultural learning within live sessions or through asynchronous material.

7th International e-Learning Excellence Awards

3. The Challenges

One of the main challenges of the project was time difference; with over 40 institutions from across the world engaging in the project and live experiences such as webinars scheduled, we understood that many events might be taking place in potentially unsociable hours for students or staff. To manage this issue, we requested partners consider the scheduling of events to suit their students but also to try to schedule at a time that would maximise participation for others.

Due to the flexibility of the Virtual World Tour, students had the option to enrol at any point, with many missing live events that had taken place previously. We had foreseen this issue and requested permission to record sessions that took place live. These recordings were then added to our Virtual World Tour hub, allowing students to watch sessions back retrospectively.

An example of webinars included:

Dr Mehal Krayem from the Centre for Social Justice and Inclusion at the University of Technology Sydney who delivered a session on 'A Brief Snapshot of Multicultural Australia'

Kathryn Engel from University of Illinois at Chicago who delivered a session on 'Applied Psychology Internships in Chicago during the Pandemic'

Heather Wheeler, Member of Parliament for South Derbyshire who delivered a session on 'Sustainable UK-Korea Relationship'.

Emma Wright and colleagues from Ryerson University in Toronto who delivered a session on 'The Diaspora of Indigenous Nationhood: from memory, place and sound'.

An additional challenge was securing a high-profile guest speaker to support with the launch of the project. Congressman Brendan F. Boyle (Conservative Representative for Philadelphia) agreed to discuss his experience and background in internationalisation. Although this was a busy election period, a date that coincided with the launch of the project was agreed, getting the project off to a fantastic start.

4. How the initiative was received

Overall, 1539 participants took part in the tour over the 4 months including 820 Coventry University students, 116 Coventry University staff and 603 external participants worldwide.

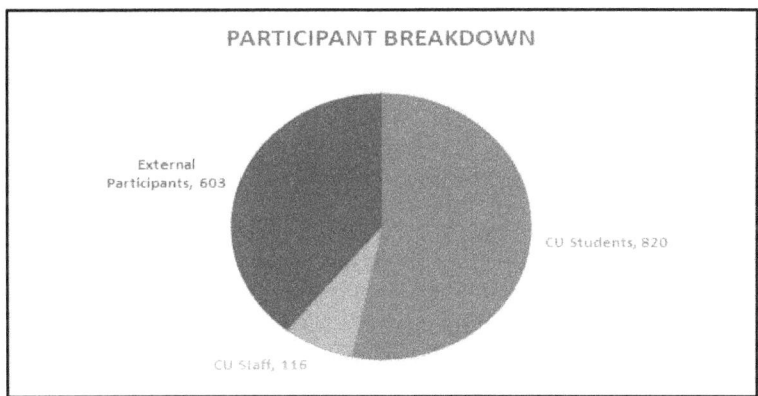

An excellent student experience and learning was a key objective of this initiative. To ensure the VWT had an impact on its participants and their learning we introduced a set of actions to collect feedback and assess achievement of international learning outcomes and project objectives.

We provided students/ participants with three international learning outcomes in line with our processes for Collaborative Online International Learning (COIL). These objectives were:

1. Gain cultural understanding from a minimum of two countries
2. Engage in one live webinar/ industry visit or retrospectively engage in one of the sessions
3. Demonstrate understanding of the UN Sustainable Development Goals (SDGs) for one of the countries on the Virtual World Tour

To successfully assess the learning outcomes, we asked students to submit a reflection and to evaluate the impact of the Virtual World Tour we used both quantitative and qualitative methods. To support the collation of data we produced an online submission form with place to submit the reflective assessment and questionnaire for students to complete.

The form contained a reflective question on each of the learning outcomes above. If students demonstrated evidence of meeting these objectives, they were awarded the COIL participation certificate. Additionally, students were asked questions based on several factors (see below).

The assessment of student reflections occurred through the project, releasing the certificates to students within a two-week time period, maintaining communication with students throughout the process. The scoring of reflections using a standardised quantitative rubric (see Appendix 1). Students had to pass all three learning outcomes to gain certification.

The qualitative method allowed us to explore the nuanced experiences of students engaged in Virtual World Tour which was crucial for the development of this innovative 'pilot' project. This also provided us with a framework to develop a better understanding including diverse perspectives which informed our further work on the project.

> 97% of those who completed the submission met the International Learning Outcomes demonstrating cultural understanding from a minimum of two countries, active engagement in activities and understanding of the UN SDG's for one of the countries on the Virtual World Tour.

Student reflections demonstrated that the emphasis on experiential internationalisation made a difference to their learning experience and the associated outcomes from their engagement.

Quotes from student reflections:

> "It's really important to learn about new cultures and overcome said intercultural barriers in order to develop one self and also to make one self-aware.
>
> I am looking forward to meeting people of new culture in my work place in the

future. I will learn to respect as well as educate myself of their culture, lifestyle, religion"

"I am a student majoring in sports management. The Olympic Games, the World Cup and other significant events are the focus of the world's attention. In the current context of globalization, sports also undertake the mission of spreading the culture of different countries. After participating in this virtual global travel, I have increased my understanding of culture. I know that the hosting of sports events must show the superiority of the local culture, and in the process, foreign tourists can break the stereotype of the country. It is a big trend to show your heritage and embrace the world at the same time, and I hope I can contribute to that. At the same time, I also realized the differences between different cultures. Such differences are a valuable asset of human society, and we need to respect them rather than demand the same human culture. The world is better because of cultural differences".

"Mexico is a country where I have learnt a lot. There was a progress in the country, which possibly is making towards the United Nations Sustainable Development Goals. I think it is very sustainable and I believe that there are areas of best practice or areas for improvement. The research on this country has made me to want to act more sustainably. I am going to try be more aware of the consequences of my actions. For these reasons, I would like to thank you for what you have done because I liked participating".

The analysis of student reflections also revealed several key takeaways that are summarised below:

- Students have enjoyed the VWT experience
- Student's learning was valuable and in line with the ILOs
- They systematically reported intercultural competence development and changes to their mind-set
- Students expressed willingness to travel and openness to undertaking international experience and interacting with diversity
- Students were very open to the use of technology and demonstrated flexibility and engagement

At the end of the project, we organised a feedback session to provide opportunity to partners and students to provide their feedback and suggestions and brainstorm ideas for next iteration of Virtual World Tour. The feedback was overwhelmingly positive with student and staff indicating willingness to contribute and/or participate. Few suggestions were made to extend the number of countries with particular suggestions of destinations; students suggested creation of more opportunities to interact with other students and requested more cultural-specific content, which was agreed as areas for development.

In addition to the reflection, the structured questionnaire asked students to rate their overall experience and number of factors.

325 Students that completed the questionnaire for the Virtual World Tour 2020, rated the overall experience 5 stars out of 5 stars (actual average figure 4.53 stars).

On average students rated the Virtual World Tour as very interesting, awarding the tour 6 out of 7 stars, (actual average figure 6.22 stars).

On average students rated the Virtual World Tour as easy to navigate and join, awarding it 6 stars out of 7, (actual average figure 5.95 stars).

On average students found that engaging in the Virtual World Tour increased their confidence in travelling to new destinations in the future, awarding the tour 6 out of 7 stars, (actual average figure 6.12 stars).

On average students found the webinars included in the Virtual World Tour interesting, and had an increased understanding of cultures, rating the tour 6 out of 7 stars, (actual average figure 6.22 stars).

4.1 Student Testimonials

As part of the evaluation stage, we also asked students to submit testimonials about their experience. Please see below examples.

Michael Chorlton - Coventry University Student

"As a keen traveller, the opportunity to engage with other cultures at Coventry University and embark on organised trips abroad was among the reasons I chose to study here. Participation in the Virtual World Tour gave me the opportunity to exercise that sense of adventure and curiosity about foreign countries in a new way. The content of the Virtual World Tour was really interesting; one week I could be discovering what high and low context cultures are on LinkedIn Learning; the next week I could be exploring what that meant in practice with students at Jiangxi University, China. I engaged with real people who were keen to share their experiences and knowledge of different countries. The ability to access the content on-demand really worked for me. Having a dull commute? Just log in and undergo a cultural learning experience about Korean food instead. Spoiler alert - it is delicious!"

Agnes Cheba Ade - Coventry University Student

"As a final year Financial Economics student and a social entrepreneur, the Virtual World Tour has been quite an enriching and exciting experience that has honestly inspired me to step up, not just as a global citizen but also as a future leader.

In addition to that, it provided me with a lot of insightful and educational content, and interesting recommendations about each of the 20+ countries we were able to explore. It gave me the opportunity to travel virtually (as many times as I wanted) and explore not just new cultures and continents, but to develop valuable employability skills and gain greater awareness of the sustainability practices in each country.

Some of my favourite destinations include Singapore, Denmark, USA, India and West Africa, where I particularly enjoyed learning about their delicious food, new languages, art, architecture, technological advancement and sustainability. All from the comfort of my house! I absolutely recommend the Virtual World Tour to anyone who wants to travel for free (turns out virtual tickets don't cost a penny), plus, you'll develop new skills including leadership and communication skills and learn about the importance and positive impact of the United Nations Sustainable Development Goals.. Do you know the only thing that can beat that? Yes, the certificate of completion! It's definitely worth joining."

Hana Ossama Nabil Ahmed - Coventry University student in Oman (partnership)

"Coventry University's Virtual World Tour is an environment to enjoy multicultural engagement and have an insight into the magical history of countries in every continent.

The Virtual World Tour, in my opinion, was a fun and new experience. Having, free access to visit all the countries around the world and learning about their history, culture, what are they famous for, their ethics and mother language. Moreover, learning how to speak new languages from different countries such as Korea, France, Spain, Malaysia, Japanese, and China. Also, gaining the understanding of policies, economy, and sustainability that each country follows.

The most exciting Virtual World Tour countries for me were Egypt, Malaysia, Belgium, France, and Indonesia. I enjoyed those because of the fun and interactive experiences such as competitions, learning about authentic history, music, and language, knowing about the famous and most recommended places to visit, and knowing the cultural dishes that I am excited to try while visiting those countries.

The Coventry University Virtual World Tour taught me how to be confident to engage and speak with new people. Lastly, I would highly recommend other students to join, participate, and attend the incredible Virtual World Tour and enjoy the experience to the fullest."

1.3 Staff Testimonials

Daniel Johnson - Lecturer in Accounting at Coventry University

"As an academic from the School of Economic Finance and Accounting and an international mobility lead, I acknowledge the significance of embracing innovative means of travelling virtually and experiencing different cultures during COVID-19 when movements are restricted. The Virtual World Tour granted me the opportunity to visit countries like South Korea, Japan, China, Malaysia, Australia and Nigeria. The trip was educative and enhanced my knowledge on economies and business developments with the impacts of pandemic. These inspiring visits wouldn't have been possible,, without the Virtual World Tour. Finally, I had the opportunity to network with partners for future collaborations. Overall, I am pleased with the organisation."

Chiara Napolitano - International Relations Coordinator at the University of Applied Sciences and Arts of Southern Switzerland

"The Virtual World Tour is an exceptional and innovative educational program that involves students and lecturers from all over the world and facilitates intercultural learning and collaboration during a time when international travel is banned. It allows participants to engage with other cultures and languages, teaching them to become better communicators and team players, as well as to gain self-awareness and cross-cultural sensitivity. At the same time, it allows them to ignite their interest and passion for future travels and international experiences, which are crucial to becoming successful professionals and global citizens. I personally participated both as a student and a lecturer, gaining insightful knowledge and learning important skills, all the while having fun and networking with students and colleagues from all around the globe."

5. Plans to further develop the initiative

It is clear that COVID-19 has affected internationalisation projects for universities. Evidence also continues to demonstrate the importance of academic and employability benefits for students who engage in international experiences.

The Virtual World Tour has shown that through collaborative approaches and engagement with universities worldwide, students can develop cultural competencies, gain new skills and build their confidence in travel.

Over 1500 participants self-enrolled to engage in a project that was not directly linked to courses or for credit, allowing us to see students and staff still had a desire to travel, network and learn despite an international pandemic.

We would encourage universities to consider virtual mobility projects to provide transformative experiences to students who are not able to travel, or during times when travel is not possible or possibly consider a blended format to enhance mobility experiences. Although we appreciate replacing the sights and feelings of travel is difficult, the Virtual World Tour was able to create new experiences and bridge the gap in supporting those that do not have the confidence or capacity to travel.

In terms of scalability, Coventry University launched its second Virtual World Tour: Continents and Cultures on 31 March 2021. The project has 45 HEIs engaged, with 967 participants. Before the new project was launched, the team took time to reflect on student feedback, and this tour provides greater opportunities for students to interact, as well as scope for students to visit more countries than previously. The new project has over 53 countries to explore with more planned before the project concludes on August 31 2021.

Promotional video: https://www.youtube.com/watch?v=ScYZTphdsRw

6. Conclusion

HEIs within the United Kingdom will have to work harder than ever before to support student engagement with international activities. COVID-19 and Brexit will present new challenges for years to come, but whilst institutions work together on Internationalisation projects like the Virtual World Tour, students can create transformational opportunities to explore new destinations safely and enrich their student experience.

Virtual mobility can be designed to be discipline specific or multidisciplinary activity, but should be inclusive to all, which is something that embodies educational policies worldwide.

This case study demonstrates clear evidence of the benefits of virtual mobility and as Coventry University aims to continue our pursuit as top UK institution for providing international experiences, where virtual mobility is a tool we will continue to use to educate students on the importance of cultural competencies and build confidence in future travel and international opportunities.

About Coventry University

Coventry University (CU) is ranked in the top 30 globally for international student engagement (2021 QS Rankings). It has been awarded five stars for international engagement by QS, won the Queen's Award for International Trade and was accorded the premiere EAIE Institutional award, all reflecting a clear global engagement strategy with exemplary outbound mobility activities embedded within it.

Comprehensive internationalisation, with mobility at its core, is at the heart of our Corporate Plan, International Strategy and Education Strategy - ensuring all students have the opportunity to become global graduates. CU has been the top UK institution for the number of international experience offered for each of the past 6 years (HESA 2014-2020). In addition, with our widening participation agenda we aim to offer all students opportunity to undertake virtual mobility and Internationalisation at Home opportunities to become global graduates

Acknowledgements

The Virtual World Tour would like to thank students and staff from the following Universities for engagement and contribution to the tour.

Austral University
Autonomous University of Madrid
California State University Long beach
City University of Hong Kong
Coventry University (Brussels Office)

Coventry University (Egypt- Knowledge Hub)
Coventry University (Wroclaw campus)
Coventry University (Singapore Hub)
Del Rosario University

Durban University of Technology
European Economic Social Committee (EESC)
Grand Canyon University
Guangdong University of Foreign Studies
Henallux Arlon, Belgium
HWR Berlin: Berlin School of Economics and Law
International College of Liberal Arts, Kofu, Japan
Institut Teknologi Sepuluh Nopember (ITS) Surabaya, Indonesia
Jiangxi University of Finance and Economics
LinkedIn Learning Solutions
Northern Arizona University
Purdue University
Radboud University Nijmegen
Ryerson University Toronto
Saint-Marie Lyon College
Southwest University of Political Science and Law
SRH Berlin University of Applied Sciences
SRH University of Heidelberg
SRM Institute of Science and Technology
Tarlac Agricultural University
The Léonard de Vinci University
The Middle East College
The Walter Sisulu University
Universidad de la Sabana
Universidad De Montevideo
Universiti Tunku Abdul Rahman
University of Brescia
University of Colima
University of Illinois at Chicago
University of Leon
University of South Florida
University of Technology Sydney
VIVES University of Applied Sciences

Author biographies

Albina Szeles is an Associate Director Global Mobility, Coventry University Group, where she leads a broad range of internationalisation and educational initiatives. Her work includes international student and staff mobility projects, internationalisation of the curriculum, creation of academic programmes, Collaborative Online International Learning and virtual mobility, partnership and business development.

Alex Regan is a Global Mobility Development Consultant, Coventry University Group, where he supports and project manages a broad range of internationalisation and educational initiatives. His work includes development of virtual mobility projects. Additionally, he has been teaching in Higher Education for 11 years and has background in Social Welfare and Sustainability.

Appendix 1
Assessment Grade Criteria: Project: The Virtual World Tour

Grade / Criteria	Fail / Referred (0-39)	Pass / Third Class (40-49)	Pass / Lower Second (50-59)	Merit / Upper Second (60-69)	Distinction / First Class (70-100)
Learning Outcome 1	Presents limited or no understanding of the topic(s). Has unsubstantiated and invalid analysis or discussion based on anecdotes and generalisation. Learning outcome not met/covered.	Shows limited understanding of the topic(s). Demonstrates basic arguments with some analysis and discussion, based on limited use of literature. Learning outcome just met/covered.	Demonstrates reasonable understanding of the topic(s). Evidence of logical and clear arguments shown in analysis and discussion, based on reasonable use of literature. Learning outcome met/covered.	Shows good understanding of the topic(s). Has well-reasoned arguments shown in analysis and discussion, based on sound use of literature. Learning outcome covered well.	Shows excellent depth and breadth of understanding of the topic(s). Presents strong and critical analysis and discussion well-grounded in literature. Learning outcome covered very comprehensively.
Learning Outcome 2	Presents limited or no understanding of the topic(s). Has unsubstantiated and invalid analysis or discussion based on anecdotes and generalisation. Learning outcome not met/covered.	Shows limited understanding of the topic(s). Demonstrates basic arguments with some analysis and discussion, based on limited use of literature. Learning outcome just met/covered.	Demonstrates reasonable understanding of the topic(s). Evidence of logical and clear arguments shown in analysis and discussion, based on reasonable use of literature. Learning outcome met/covered.	Shows good understanding of the topic(s). Has well-reasoned arguments shown in analysis and discussion, based on sound use of literature. Learning outcome covered well.	Shows excellent clear depth and breadth of understanding of the topic(s). Presents strong and critical analysis and discussion well-grounded in literature. Learning outcome covered very comprehensively.
Learning Outcome 3	Presents limited or no understanding of the topic(s). Has unsubstantiated and invalid analysis or discussion based on anecdotes and generalisation. Learning outcome not met/covered.	Shows limited understanding of the topic(s). Demonstrates basic arguments with some analysis and discussion, based on limited use of literature. Learning outcome just met/covered.	Demonstrates reasonable understanding of the topic(s). Evidence of logical and clear arguments shown in analysis and discussion, based on reasonable use of literature. Learning outcome met/covered.	Shows good understanding of the topic(s). Has well-reasoned arguments shown in analysis and discussion, based on sound use of literature. Learning outcome covered well.	Shows excellent clear depth and breadth of understanding of the topic(s). Presents strong and critical analysis and discussion well-grounded in literature. Learning outcome covered very comprehensively.

www.ingramcontent.com/pod-product-compliance
Lightning Source LLC
Chambersburg PA
CBHW060824190426
43197CB00038B/2413